THE ROUGH GUIDE to

New Zealand
off the beaten track

Rough Guides Online
www.roughguides.com

Rough Guide credits

Author: Paul Whitfield
Editor: Helena Smith
Typesetting: Peter Buckley
Production: Katherine Owers
Cartography: Katie Lloyd-Jones
Proofreader: Susannah Wight
Cover: Peter Buckley
Project Manager: Philippa Hopkins

Project facilitated by Remote World Ltd.

Cover picture: "Lake Mapourika, Westland"
Julian Apse (www.julianapse.co.nz)

Published by Rough Guides Ltd,
80 Strand, London WC2R 0RL
© Rough Guides Ltd, 2006

ISBN: 1-84353-746-X
Printed in Italy by Legoprint S.p.A.

Introduction

C ast away in the middle of the South Pacific, some 1500km east of Australia, is the magnificent landscape of **New Zealand**. It is a unique land packed with wonderful raw scenery and known by its people as "Godzone" (God's own country). This is a country defined by craggy coastlines, sweeping beaches, primeval forests, snow-capped alpine mountains, bubbling volcanic pools, fast-flowing rivers and glacier-fed lakes – all largely unfettered by the crowds you so often find elsewhere. Of course it also has vibrant and cosmopolitan cities, but New Zealand is the perfect place to get **off the beaten track**.

In the mythology of its indigenous **Maori** people, New Zealand was fished from the depths of the ocean floor by the fearless warrior, Maui. Its natural beauty, like all of creation, was the product of careful nursing by the gods. The Maori called the land **Aotearoa** – the Land of the Long White Cloud – which is exactly what it must have seemed to their ancestors from the South Pacific around 800 years ago.

Aeons of isolated evolution without humans (or any other land mammals) had allowed New Zealand's fauna to develop in unusual ways, with **birds** adapting to exploit almost every niche in the environment. The kiwi is well known but there are equally curious birds such as the kakapo (the world's

---

To call any **telephone number** in this guide from the UK, dial 0064 followed by number minus its initial 0.

All prices in this guide are given in **New Zealand dollars**. Currently £1 buys NZ$2.8.

Useful websites: Tourism New Zealand ⓦ www.newzealand.com and The Department of Conservation ⓦ www.doc.govt.nz.

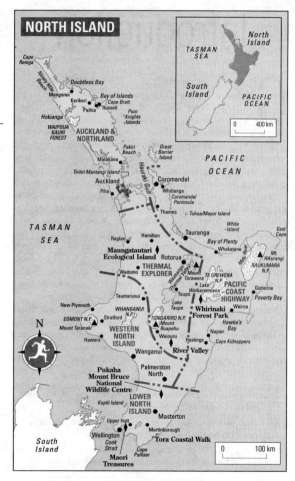

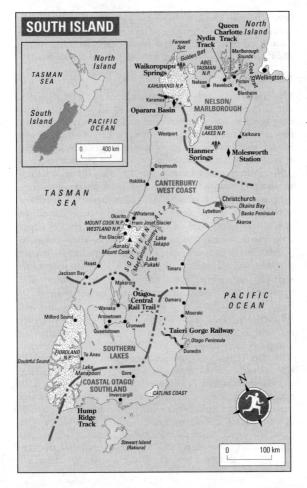

largest parrot), the kea (an alpine parrot) and the ungainly takahe, which was thought extinct for fifty years. You can catch a glimpse of these and many others at some of the island sanctuaries and nature reserves around the country.

Where to go

The country comprises two main islands and a third smaller one at its southern tip. The **North Island** is home to stunning beaches, kauri forests, caves and phenomenal geothermal activity. Maori culture is strongest here. On the **South Island**, the focus is on grand mountain scenery, adventure activities, historic architecture and wildlife encounters.

All of this provides a canvas for boundless diversions, from strolls along windswept beaches and multi-day tramps (hikes) over alpine passes to the adrenalin-charged **adventure activities** of bungy jumping and whitewater rafting. In fact, some visitors take on New Zealand as a kind of large-scale assault course, aiming to tackle as many adventures as possible in the time available. But gentler pursuits are readily available, too, throughout the country, whether your tastes take you on an exploration of some of the country's best **vineyards** and innovative **restaurants**, or on quiet walks beside turquoise lakes or deep into the bush. The cities add another dimension, exposing you to the cultural diversity of New Zealand, a vigorous mix largely the product of European and Maori heritage.

Tourism is big business here, but even the key destinations – Queenstown and Rotorua, for example – only seem busy and commercialized in comparison with the low-key Kiwi norm. What's more, everything is easily accessible, packed into a land area little larger than Britain that has a population of just 4.1 million, over half of which is tucked away in the three largest cities: Auckland, the capital Wellington and Christchurch. Elsewhere, you can travel for miles through steep-hilled farmland and rarely see a soul, and there are even remote spots which, it's reliably contended, no human has ever visited.

When to go

Choosing when to go is largely a matter of balancing the weather with a desire to avoid the busiest season, though you might also be influenced by some of the **events** and **festivals** listed on pp.92–96.

Since the Maori named New Zealand the Land of the Long White Cloud, **climate** has been of paramount importance to its people, many of whom make their living from the land. New Zealand has mild temperatures, moderately

	Jan	Feb	Mar	Apr	May	Jun	Jul	Aug	Sep	Oct	Nov	Dec
Auckland												
av. max. temp. (°C)	23	23	22	19	17	14	13	14	16	17	19	21
av. min. temp. (°C)	16	16	15	13	11	9	8	8	9	11	12	14
av. rainfall (mm)	79	94	81	97	112	137	145	117	102	102	89	79
Napier												
av. max. temp. (°C)	24	23	22	19	17	14	13	14	17	19	21	23
av. min. temp. (°C)	14	14	13	10	8	5	5	6	7	9	11	13
av. rainfall (mm)	74	76	74	76	89	86	102	84	56	56	61	58
Wellington												
av. max. temp. (°C)	21	21	19	17	14	13	12	12	14	16	17	19
av. min. temp. (°C)	13	13	12	11	8	7	6	6	8	9	10	12
av. rainfall (mm)	81	81	81	97	117	117	137	117	97	102	89	89
Christchurch												
av. max. temp. (°C)	21	21	19	17	13	11	10	11	14	17	19	21
av. min. temp. (°C)	12	12	10	7	4	2	2	2	4	7	8	11
av. rainfall (mm)	56	43	48	48	66	66	69	48	46	43	48	56
Hokitika												
av. max. temp. (°C)	19	19	18	16	14	12	12	12	13	15	16	18
av. min. temp. (°C)	12	12	11	8	6	3	3	3	6	8	9	11
av. rainfall (mm)	262	191	239	236	244	231	218	239	226	292	267	262
Queenstown												
av. max. temp. (°C)	21	21	20	15	11	9	9	11	14	18	19	20
av. min. temp. (°C)	10	10	9	7	3	1	0	1	3	5	7	10
av. rainfall (mm)	79	72	74	72	64	58	59	63	66	77	64	62
Dunedin												
av. max. temp. (°C)	19	19	17	15	12	9	9	11	13	15	17	18
av. min. temp. (°C)	10	10	9	7	5	4	3	3	5	6	7	9
av. rainfall (mm)	86	71	76	71	81	81	79	76	69	76	81	89

Fact file

• Adrift in the south Pacific Ocean some 1500km east of Australia, New Zealand is one of the most isolated major land masses and was the last to be populated, less than 1000 years ago.

• At 268,000 square kilometres in area, New Zealand is a little larger than the UK and with just over 4 million people, most parts of the country are thinly populated.

• New Zealand is very physically varied, with hairline fiords and glacier-weighted mountains in the south; rolling green hills fringed with golden beaches in the north; and abundant volcanic activity producing geysers and natural hot pools.

• For an instinctively conservative nation, New Zealand has often been socially progressive. There is a growing "knowledge economy" and in recent years tourism has become the biggest sector of the economy.

• Godzone has 40 million sheep. That's ten for every inhabitant, down from twenty to one in the early 1980s. New Zealand's economy has traditionally been agricultural, and dairy products, meat and wool remain central to its continued prosperity, with forestry and fishing also playing a part.

• New Zealand's flora and fauna developed independently, giving rise to a menagerie of exotica: tall tree ferns, an alpine parrot (kea), a huge ground-dwelling parrot (kakapo), the odd-ball kiwi, and many more.

high rainfall and many hours of sunshine. In general, the west of the country receives the brunt of the prevailing westerlies and is wetter – indeed, Fiordland is one of the wettest places on earth. The eastern sides of both the main islands are in the rain shadow and are generally drier.

Summer generally runs from December to March and is when most visitors arrive. That alone is good reason to travel either in **spring** (Sept to Nov) or **autumn** (April and May). Even **winter** (June to Aug) doesn't present too much hardship, and skiing is added to the mix of adventure activities.

Ten things not to miss

The Bridge to Nowhere (see p.48). Jetboat or kayak through the gorgeous Whanganui National Park to reach the concrete span that recalls abandoned farming hopes in this remote region.

Hokianga Harbour (see p.29). Huge sand dunes overlooking a peaceful harbour, with easy access to New Zealand's largest kauri trees.

Martinborough (p.53). Boutique wineries crowd in on this diminutive town, making walking tours (with Pinot Noir sampling) a real pleasure.

Queen Charlotte Track (see p.61). See some of New Zealand's best coastal scenery on this wonderful track, with classy accommodation and your bags carried for you by boat.

Stewart Island (see p.88). Over 85 percent of New Zealand's third island is national park, and there's no better place for seeing kiwi in the wild.

Wanaka canyoning (see p.78). Deep gorges near Wanaka make some of the best terrain for canyoning: the best fun you can have with a wetsuit on.

White Island (see p.37). Cruise to a live volcanic island that's often so active you have to don a gas mask to peer into the steaming crater.

Surfing at Raglan (see p.32). Rows of immaculate waves appear like blue corduroy at the left-hand breaks of Whale Bay and Manu Bay, just outside the surfie resort town of Raglan.

Otago Central Rail Trail (see p.79). Two or three days on a bike is the best way to tackle this 150km former rail route through the gorgeous open valleys and craggy hills of the Maniototo region.

The Oparara Basin (see p.71). Gorgeous limestone scenery, a magical cave tour and a new mountain bike track make this quiet but up-and-coming area a real treasure.

Getting there

New Zealand is the perfect destination for travelling independently and seeking the advice of a destination expert such as **Trailfinders** (⊛www.trailfinders.com; ☎0845/050 5921) is advised. Trailfinders can help you with bookings for accommodation, self-drive itineraries, escorted tours and car and motorhome hire.

Flying to New Zealand almost always involves **scheduled flights**. Airfares depend on the season, with fares highest over summer and dropping from May to October. The main international gateway to New Zealand is Auckland International Airport in the north of the North Island, while Christchurch Airport is the main entry point in the South Island. An **open-jaw ticket** (which involves flying into one airport and out of the other), usually costs no more than an ordinary return and means not retracing your steps to get out of the country.

If New Zealand is only one stop on a longer journey, you might consider buying a **Round-the-World** (**RTW**) ticket, usually valid for a year. Some travel agents can sell you an "off-the-shelf" RTW ticket that will have you touching down in about half a dozen cities (Auckland is on many itineraries); others will assemble a route for you, tailored to your needs, though this will be more expensive.

Air New Zealand (⊛www.airnewzealand.co.uk, ☎0800/028 4149; or visit the Air New Zealand Travelcentre, New Zealand House, 80 Haymarket, London SW1Y 4TE) operates daily flights from London Heathrow to Auckland and offers connections to 25 domestic destinations around the country if you buy an international ticket with them. Optional stopovers in the Pacific Islands (Tahiti, Fiji, Cook Islands, Tonga and Samoa) are also available. Air New Zealand has recently introduced a new Pacific Premium Economy cabin – the only airline to offer premium economy seats on flights to and from New Zealand – and from the 29th

October 2006 they will be flying from Heathrow to NZ via Hong Kong, making them the only airline to fly right around the world (They go via LA the other way). There will be two flights a day, and a return ticket will allow you to go out via LA and back via Hong Kong (or any permutation of the two routes) if you wish.

Getting around

New Zealand is a relatively small country and getting around is easy, with some form of transport going to most destinations, though often you may be limited to one or two services per day.

Internal **flights** are relatively cheap if bought well in advance, but with time to spare you will appreciate the scenery better by travelling at ground level. For getting off the beaten track, you'll need a car. **Rental cars** can be surprisingly cheap if you shop around, and are cheaper still if the hire period extends over a month.

The **rail** service is very limited and is also quite expensive, while competition on the **ferries** connecting the North and South Islands keeps them good value. The cheapest way to get around is by **coach** or shuttle bus though it can be time-consuming. And with such stunning countryside, **cycling** is an increasingly popular option.

You'll still need to take to the air or the water (or go hiking) to reach the offshore islands and the remoter parts of the main islands that remain stubbornly impenetrable by road.

Domestic flights

Many visitors fly into Auckland at the beginning of their trip and out again from either Christchurch or Wellington at the end, so the Christchurch to Auckland leg is the only **domestic flight** they take. Those with a tight timetable wanting to hit a few key sights in a short time might be tempted by some good value internal fares, the product of a reasonable amount of competition.

By far the biggest domestic airline operator in New Zealand is **Air New Zealand** (☎0800/737 000, ⊕www.airnewzealand.co.nz), which serves all the main centres and numerous minor ones – 25 destinations in all. The main competition is from **Origin Pacific** (☎0800/302 302, ⊕www.originpacific.co.nz), with frequent flights to ten cities, and **Qantas** (☎0800/808 767, ⊕www.qantas.co.nz), which serves Auckland, Wellington, Christchurch, Rotorua and Queenstown.

Driving and vehicle rental

Driving is a very popular way to get around New Zealand. You drive on the left and road rules are similar to the UK, so there should be few problems. **Road conditions** are generally good, though some rental companies prohibit the use of their vehicles on the worst gravel roads. You'll get good **car rental** deals from the major international companies, and even cheaper rates from local firms. The best bet is to go for mid-range firms rather than those that appear to offer rock-bottom rates. Prices are highest from December to February. A medium-sized four-door sedan will go for $40–90 a day in summer, and one-way rentals usually incur a substantial drop-off fee.

Campervans are also very popular. No special licence is required, and you'll have the freedom to drive around the country staying in campgrounds and sneaking the odd free night in wayside rest areas. This isn't strictly legal but you're unlikely to be hassled in isolated areas. Expect to pay $70–150 a day for something suitable for two adults in summer.

If you're staying in the country for a couple of months, **buying a used car** can be cost-effective as reselling can recoup enough of the price to make it cheaper than using public transport or renting. Backpacker hostel noticeboards are the best hunting grounds.

Trains

Only three **train** services still operate in New Zealand, all run primarily for tourists. They're operated by **Tranz Scenic** (®www.tranzscenic.co.nz) who run one train a day between Auckland and Wellington and one between Picton and Christchurch. They also operate one of the best scenic rail journeys in the world, the **TranzAlpine** – from Christchurch over the Southern Alps to Greymouth. For the best prices on all tickets you'll need to book in advance. Tranz Scenic's **Scenic Rail Pass** gives unlimited travel on Trans Scenic trains for either a week ($299), or a month ($499). The one-week pass includes one Interislander ferry passage between the North and South islands; the one-month pass allows two crossings.

In addition there are several privately run trains, the best being the Driving Creek Railway (see p.37) and the Taieri Gorge Railway (see p.34).

Buses

Buses services are generally cheap, reliable and comfortable, though many routes have only one or two buses a day in each direction. The only nationwide network is jointly run by **InterCity** (®www.intercitycoach.co.nz) and **Newmans** (®www.newmanscoach.co.nz), who operate an integrated timetable and booking system.

Fares vary according to the popularity of a particular service, and there is a variety of passes and excursions that will get you to all major destinations. **Shuttle-bus** companies fill in the gaps around the country, usually operating smaller and more nimble minibuses. They cover many of the same routes (often faster) but also run more obscure routes that take you off the beaten track. Their fares are usually fixed and travel passes are not available. Visitor centres carry timetables, so you can compare destinations and fares.

Backpacker buses

Backpacker buses combine the flexibility of independent travel with the convenience of a tour. You purchase a ticket for a fixed route, then either stick with your bus or stay in some places longer and hop on a later one. The ticket doesn't cover food, accommodation or activities, though the latter are often arranged and discounted.

The best deals are with the **Magic Travellers Network** (@www.magicbus.co.nz), which targets independent travellers. The very popular **Kiwi Experience** (@www.kiwiexperience.com) has more of a party reputation, and **Stray** (@www.straytravel.co.nz) is carving out a similar niche.

Ferries

There are no bridges between any of New Zealand's three main islands, so to get between them you'll need to travel by **ferry** – generally a very pleasant and scenic experience (see p.56).

Two companies ply Cook Strait between Wellington on the North Island and Picton on the South Island, a three-hour trip. **Interislander** (@www.interislander.co.nz) and **Blue Bridge** (@www.bluebridge.co.nz) both operate comfortable vehicle and passenger ferries year round, though bad weather does sometimes halt services. Blue Bridge has relatively low fixed fares while Interislander offers discounts for advance purchases: book at least a month in advance if possible. Most car rental companies don't allow rentals on the ferries, but they do have a pick-up place for rentals on both sides of Cook Strait.

Ferries also allow you to get off the main tourist trail. Stewart Island Experience (@www.stewartislandexperience.co.nz) sails daily between **Bluff** at the southern tip of the South Island and Stewart Island. It can be a rough trip but the destination is rewarding.

You'll use ferries to access the islands of Auckland's Hauraki Gulf, notably Rangitoto, Great Barrier and Tiritiri Matangi islands. Elsewhere, **cruise boats** take you on all manner of whale-watching, dolphin-swimming and sightseeing cruises, and you may even have recourse to a **water taxi** to take you out to some idyllic Marlborough Sounds lodge that's inaccessible by road.

Accommodation

Accommodation will take up a fair chunk of your budget, but the expense is ameliorated by excellent standards. Finding accommodation is only a problem during the peak season (Dec to Feb) in the main resorts.

Kiwis travel widely at home, most choosing to self-cater at the country's huge number of well-equipped **holiday parks** (aka motor camps or just campgrounds) and **motels**, shunning **hotels**, which cater mainly to package holidaymakers and the business community. An appealing alternative is the range of **guesthouses**, **B&Bs**, **homestays**, **farmstays** and **lodges**, which cover everything from a room in someone's suburban home to pampered luxury in a country mansion.

Wherever you stay, you can expect unstinting hospitality and a truckload of advice on local activities and onward travel. As far as **facilities** go, there is almost always some

Information

The primary sources of objective information in New Zealand are the countrywide i-SITE visitor information centres found in most cities and wherever tourists congregate. They're open seven days a week, handle accommodation reservations and can book transport and tours. Most of the businesses they recommend bear the Qualmark™ quality standard, indicating that they have been independently assessed. Accommodation additionally gets a star rating from one ("acceptable"; rarely used) to five ("exceptional").

form of laundry and low-cost Internet access, and tea and coffee are often provided free.

Hotels and motels

In the cities and major resorts, you'll find a range of **hotels** including many of the international chains. They usually charge $150–300 a room, though at quiet times and weekends there can be substantial discounts; it's always worth asking.

Most Kiwi families on the move prefer the astonishingly well-equipped **motels**, which congregate along the roads running into town. They come with bed linen, towels, bathroom, a full kitchen and tea and coffee. Rooms range from all-in-one studios ($70–100 for two people), with beds, kettle, toaster and a microwave; through one-bedroom units ($100–120), usually with a full and separate kitchen; to two- and three-bedroom suites, sleeping six or eight. Suites generally go for the same basic price as a one-bedroom unit, with each additional adult paying $15–25, making them an economical choice for groups travelling together.

B&Bs, lodges and boutique hotels

While families may prefer the freedom and adaptability of a motel, couples are generally better served by a **bed and breakfast** (B&B). This might be a simple room with a bathroom down the hall and a modest continental breakfast included in the price. But the term also encompasses luxurious colonial homes with well-furnished en-suite rooms and sumptuous home-cooked breakfasts. Those at the top end are now fashioning themselves as **lodges**, **boutique hotels** and "exclusive retreats", where standards of service and comfort are raised to extraordinary levels.

Roughly speaking, **rates** for a double room are $80–150 at B&Bs, $150–300 at boutique hotels and reach stratospheric levels when it comes to the exclusive retreats. Rates drop in the low season, when these places can often be exceptionally good value.

Homestays and farmstays

Homestays usually offer a guest room or two in an ordinary house where you join the owners for breakfast – an excellent way to meet ordinary New Zealanders. It is courteous to **call in advance**, and bear in mind you'll usually have to **pay in cash**. Rural versions often operate as **farmstays**, where you're encouraged to stay a couple of nights and are welcome to spend the intervening day trying your hand at farm tasks: rounding up sheep, milking cows or fencing. Both homestays and farmstays charge $80–120 for a double room, including breakfast.

Hostels, backpackers and YHAs

New Zealand is awash with around four hundred budget and self-catering places, known as either **hostels** or **backpackers**, and offering a bed or bunk for $18–25. They're frequently in superb locations – bang in the centre of town, beside the beach, or amid magnificent scenery – and are great places to meet others and hook up to the travellers' grapevine. You'll typically find a fully equipped kitchen, laundry, TV, Internet access, and perhaps a pool, barbecue area, bike and/or canoe rental and information on local work opportunities.

Many hostels allow you to pitch a tent in the grounds for $12–15 a person, and most have double, twin and family **rooms** ($20–30 per adult), the more expensive ones with en-suite bathrooms.

Around 60 places are classified as **YHA hostels**, which maintain a predominance of single-sex dorms. YHAs are outnumbered six to one by other backpacker hostels, where the atmosphere is more variable: some are friendly and relaxed, others are more party-oriented. Most are aligned with the New Zealand-based Budget Backpacker Hostels, and are listed (along with current prices) in the **BBH** accommodation guide, widely available from hostels and visitor centres.

Motorcamps, campsites and cabins

New Zealand has some of the world's best **camping** facilities, so even if you've never been camping before you may
well find yourself using a **holiday park**, also known as a
motor camp. There's space to pitch tents ($12–15 per per-
son), hook-ups for campervans ($25–35 per van) and usually
a broad range of dorms ($20–25 per person), cabins and
motel units ($40–100 for two). Elsewhere you'll find more
down-to-earth camping at wonderfully located Department
of Conservation sites ($5–10 per person).

Camping is best from November to May, but can be OK at
any time of the year. Tents will need a fly sheet to repel the
worst that the elements can dish out, and an inner tent with
bug-proof ventilation for hot mornings.

Auckland and Northland

For the majority of international visitors, the point of arrival in New Zealand is **Auckland**, New Zealand's largest city with around 1.3 million people (almost a third of the nation's total). It enjoys a terrific setting, straddling the North Island's "wasp waist" with the Manukau Harbour and surf-pounded beaches to the west, and the island-studded waters of the Hauraki Gulf to the east.

The arrival of immigrants from Tonga, Samoa and other South Pacific islands in the 1960s and 1970s made this the largest **Polynesian** settlement in the world, and recent immigration from south and east Asia means it is now the most multicultural of New Zealand's cities. Auckland certainly has its urban attractions, with fine museums and art galleries, a lively restaurant scene and even a handful of adventure activities, but dig a little deeper and it's possible to get well off the beaten track.

The slender finger of land protruding north from Auckland is **Northland**, one of the most traditional Maori regions of all Aotearoa's provinces and the cradle of early contact between Maori and the first Europeans. Scenically, Northland splits down the middle. The **east coast** comprises a labyrinth of straggling peninsulas, with hidden coves between plunging headlands. There could hardly be a greater contrast than with the **west coast**, one enormous dune-backed beach pounded by powerful Tasman breakers and punctuated by occasional harbours. Here the main draws are the watery pleasures of the Bay of Islands and the long drive up Ninety Mile Beach to the northern tip, Cape Reinga. Many make a quick trip round in three or four days, missing out on some lesser-known wonders.

West Coast beaches

40km west of Auckland City. Arataki Visitor Centre Sept–April daily 9am–5pm; May–Aug Mon–Fri 10am–4pm, Sat & Sun 9am–5pm.

Auckland's western limit is defined by the bush-clad **Waitakere Ranges**, which rise up to five hundred metres. The western slopes roll down to the wild, black-sand **west coast beaches**. Pounded by heavy surf and punctuated by precipitous headlands, these tempestuous shores are a perfect counterpoint to the calm, gently shelving beaches and islands of the Hauraki Gulf to the east.

The easiest access to the majority of the walks and beaches is the **Waitakere Scenic Drive** (Route 24), which winds through the ranges past the informative Arataki visitor centre. A felled kauri has been transformed by the local Maori carvers into a striking pou, or guardian post, which marks the entrance and sets the tone for several smaller carvings within. Outside, walkways forge into the second-growth forest: the ten-minute plant identification loop trail identifies a dozen or so significant forest trees and ferns, while a longer trail (1hr 15min) visits one of the few mature kauri stands to survive the loggers' onslaught.

One of the best of the black-sand beaches is **Karekare**. In one hectic year, this dramatic spot was jolted out of its relative obscurity, providing the setting for the beach scenes in Jane Campion's 1993 film *The Piano* and, at much the same time, the inspiration for the New Zealand band Crowded House's *Together Alone* album. Kauri loggers once built a railway along the coast here, and spikes driven into the rocky headland can still be seen on the easy **Gap Gallery Track**.

Immediately north is **Piha**, the quintessential West Coast surf beach with its string of low-key weekend cottages now being eased out by swanky new commuter homes. The three-kilometre-long sweep of beach is split by Piha's defining feature, 101-metre **Lion Rock**. With some imagination, this former Maori *pa* (fortified site) resembles a seated lion staring out to sea; the energetic climb to a shoulder two-thirds of the way up (20–30min return) is best done as the day cools and the sun casts a gentler light. If you choose to take a dip, be sure to **swim between the flags** staked out by the surf lifesaving club, as the currents are very strong.

The Tasman surf also pounds the coast at **Muriwai**, chiefly notable for the **gannet colony** which occupies Otakamiro Point and Motutara Island just offshore. The gannets breed here between September and March before migrating to sunnier Australian climes, a few staying behind with the fur seals which inhabit the rocks below. Gannets normally prefer the protection of islands and this is one of the few places where they nest on the mainland, in this case right below some excellent viewing platforms from where you can observe them gracefully wheeling on the up-draughts.

Tiritiri Matangi

30km north of Auckland. Day-trips by ferry (3–5 weekly; $46 return) from Auckland Ferry Terminal with Kawau Kat ☎0800/888 006, ⓦwww.kawaukat.co.nz.

No one with even the vaguest interest in New Zealand's wonderful birdlife should pass up the opportunity to visit **Tiritiri Matangi**, a low island run as an "open sanctuary". Visitors are free to roam through the predator-free bush where, within a couple of hours, it's quite possible to see **endangered native birds** (see box, p.87) such as taka-he, saddlebacks, whiteheads, red-crowned parakeets, North Island robins, kokako and brown teals.

Once farmed, the island became uneconomic in the 1970s

and was singled out as a prime site for helping to restore bird populations. Since 1984, a **reforestation programme** has seen the planting of over 300,000 saplings, almost all raised from seeds found on the island. Though the rapidly regenerating bush is still far from mature, the birds are thriving with the aid of feeding stations to supplement diet in the leaner months, and nesting boxes standing in for decaying trees.

Four of the species released here are among the rarest in the world, with total populations of around a couple of hundred. The most visible are the flightless **takahe**, lumbering blue-green turkey-sized birds long thought to be extinct. **Northern blue penguins** also frequent Tiritiri and can be seen all year round, but are most in evidence in March when they come ashore to moult, and from September to December when they nest in specially constructed viewing boxes located along the seashore path just west of the main wharf. To stand a chance of seeing the **little-spotted kiwi** and tuatara you'll have to be here overnight in a self-contained bunkhouse (call the rangers on ☎09/476 0010; $20 per person).

Great Barrier Island

Access by daily ferry and plane. For information contact the island visitor centre ☎09/429 0033, ⓦwww.greatbarrier.co.nz.

Just two hours by ferry from Auckland, rugged and sparsely populated **Great Barrier Island** is a world apart. It seems almost anachronistic in its lack of mains electricity or a reticulated water supply and retains a sense of peace and detachment unique to island life. There are no towns to speak of, no industry and no regular public transport, but you'll find plenty of **beaches**, some **hot springs**, deep indented **harbours** and tightly packed **mountains** clad in luxuriant bush.

The island's kauri trees were once logged and there was even a short-lived whaling station in the 1950s, but by the

1960s Great Barrier was attracting alternative lifestylers. Much of the Seventies idealism has been supplanted by a more modern pragmatism, but **self-sufficiency** remains. Many people grow their own vegetables, everyone has their own water supply and the load on diesel generators is eased by wind-driven turbines and solar panels.

With no real must-see attractions, Great Barrier relies on its laid-back charm. Many come for a couple of days lying on **Medlands Beach**, perhaps doing some surfing or body boarding. Others focus on strolling along some easy paths and wallowing in the **Kaitoke Hot Springs** which well up in a stream surrounded by boardwalks. Some come to hike the mountainous trails around the 621-metre **Hirakimata** (Mount Hobson), and spend the night in a basic hut of one of the fine, simple campgrounds. If fresh fish and seafood ring your bell, then Great Barrier is hard to beat for fishing and diving, best conducted with one of the charter boat operators.

Most people **stay** two or three nights here, easily done with a decent selection of backpackers, lodges and swanky retreats.

Matakana, Leigh and Goat Island

Around 70km north of Auckland and 10–25km northeast of Warkworth. Morris & James Mon–Fri 8.30am–4.30pm, Sat & Sun 10am–5pm; free. Herons' Flight daily from 10am ☎09/422 7915, ⓦwww.heronsflight.co.nz. Goat Island Dive, 142a Pakiri Rd Mon–Fri 9am–5pm, Sat & Sun 8am–5pm ☎0800/348 369 & 09/422 6925, ⓦwww.goatislanddive.co.nz.

Matakana is little more than a road junction at the heart of a fledgling wine-making region, though the surrounding area is dotted with the workshops of craftspeople. Indeed the region is booming, and hundreds flock to the weekly

Farmers' Market (Sat 8am–1pm).

The catalyst for the region's development was the **Morris & James Pottery & Tileworks**, 2km from Matakana village at Tongue Farm Road, which in the late 1970s exploited New Zealand's fortress economy by producing otherwise unobtainable handmade terracotta tiles and large garden pots made from local clay. You can catch a free 30min tour of the pottery (Mon–Fri 11.30am) before a visit to the pleasant café-bar.

Despite received wisdom about high humidity and proximity to the sea being unsuitable for viticulture, half the valley seems to have been planted with **vineyards** during the last decade or so. Pick up the free Matakana Coast Wine Country booklet and follow it to Heron's Flight, 49 Sharp Rd, where Sangiovese, Pinotage and Chardonnay have been planted with considerable success. At the lovely **restaurant** overlooking the vines, try an antipasto platter ($18) and don't miss the delicious Sangiovese grape juice.

East of Matakana, the road runs 13km to the village of **Leigh**, its picturesque harbour bobbing with wooden fishing boats. The boats attest to the abundance of fish where ocean currents meet the waters of the Hauraki Gulf, but overfishing has taken its toll. This underlines the importance of the **Cape Rodney–Okakari Marine Reserve**, 4km northeast of Leigh, which is usually known simply as **Goat Island** for the bush-clad islet 300m offshore. Established in 1975, this was New Zealand's first marine reserve, stretching 5km along the shoreline and 800m off the coast. Three angling-and shellfishing-free decades later, the undersea life is thriving, with large rock lobster and huge snapper. Feeding is discouraged – blue maomaos in particular developed a taste for frozen peas and used to mob swimmers and divers.

Easy access to the beach (right by the road-end parking area), wonderfully clear water, rock pools on wave-cut platforms, a variety of undersea terrains and relatively benign currents combine to make this an enormously popular year-round **diving** spot, as well as a favourite summer destination for families: aim to come midweek if you value tranquillity. In fine weather (Sept–April only), join the 45-minute **glass-bottomed boat tours** around the island ($20), which depart from the beach.

   Snorkellers enjoy a lush world of kelp forest with numerous multicoloured fish, while those who venture deeper will find more exposed seascapes with an abundance of sponges. Throughout summer there's a kiosk beside the beach renting basic snorkelling gear at $10 for a couple of hours, $15 all day. For anything more sophisticated visit the highly professional Goat Island Dive, who rent gear for similar prices (plus full dive gear with two tanks for $90) year round.

Pakiri Beach

30km northeast of Warkworth. Pakiri Beach Horse Riding, Rahuikiri Road, Pakiri Beach ☎09/422 6275, ⊛www.horseride-nz.co.nz.

North of Leigh, a sealed road continues 10km to the tiny community of **Pakiri**, with its long, dune-backed white strand. It's a gorgeous beach with good surf, but the main attraction here is **horse-riding**, with the highly professional Pakiri Beach Horse Riding, who operate year-round and run a great café. Rides range from a brief jaunt along the beach and through a pohutukawa (a red flowering tree, often refered to as the "New Zealand Christmas Tree") glade to multi-day safaris through stands of native bush and along the tops of seacliffs. Outings leave daily at 10am & 2pm, and there are three more departures in the peak summer season for the two-hour rides ($80) and half-day rides ($95). Overnight trips start at $450 and range up to the epic seven-day Coast-to-Coast ride ($2995; book months in advance).

   There's good reason to stay over in a range of attractive **accommodation**: riverside backpacker cabins, self-contained beachside cabins for two people, and a luxurious four-bedroom beach house for up to eight.

Poor Knights Islands

25km off the east coast of Northland, 180km north of Auckland. Visit with Dive Tutukaka ☎0800/288 882 & 09/434 3867, ⓦwww.diving.co.nz; two-dive day trips with all gear $200.

Jacques Cousteau apparently claimed that the **Poor Knights Islands Marine Reserve** is one of the ten best dive spots in the world. The warm ocean currents from the north and lack of run-off from the land combine to create wonderfully clear water – **visibility** approaches 30m most of the year, though in spring (roughly Oct–Dec) plankton can reduce it to 15–20m.

These waters are home to New Zealand's most diverse range of sea life, including a few subtropical species found nowhere else, as well as a striking underwater landscape of near-vertical rock faces that drop almost 100m through a labyrinth of caves, fissures and **rock arches** teeming with rainbow-coloured fish, crabs, soft corals, kelp forests and shellfish. The Poor Knights also lie along the migratory routes of a number of **whale** species, so blue, humpback, sei

Marine reserves and diving in NZ

New Zealand has done a pretty good job of protecting its land. A third of the total surface area is protected in some form of National Park or reserve. But things aren't so rosy around the coast where only one percent of New Zealand's territorial waters are protected. The government has committed to upping the quota. The first no-extraction Marine Reserve was established in 1975. Controversial at the time, it is now widely applauded even by fishers who have noticed improved fishing in areas immediately bordering the reserve. Of course, snorkellers and scuba divers were in hog heaven, and New Zealand has gradually established itself as something of a dive mecca. And probably the biggest draw of all is the Poor Knights Islands.

and minke whales, as well as dolphins, are not uncommon. As if that weren't enough, the waters north and south of the reserve are home to two navy **wrecks**, both deliberately scuttled. The survey ship HMNZS *Tui* was sunk in 1999 to form an artificial reef, and such was its popularity with divers and marine life that the obsolete frigate *Waikato* followed two years later.

Cape Brett and the Cape Brett Track

Bay of Island, 250km north of Auckland. Cape Brett Walkways
℡09/403 8823, ⓦwww.capebrettwalks.co.nz.

The Bay of Islands is one of New Zealand's tourist hot spots, famed for its cruises, dolphin swimming trips, diving and big-game fishing. Much of this activity relies on calm waters created by the nurturing arm of **Cape Brett** which protects the region from swells from the south and east. Most visitors fleetingly see Cape Brett on cruises to the **Hole in the Rock**, a tunnel-pierced island off the tip of the peninsula, but it rewards a more leisurely inspection.

About the best overnight tramp in Northland is the challenging but rewarding **Cape Brett Track** (20km; 6–8hr each way), which follows the hilly ridge along the centre of the peninsula with sea occasionally visible on both sides. The track crosses private land, so all walkers must pay a track fee ($30, payable in advance). The Cape Brett lighthouse at the tip of the peninsula is now automatic but was once tended by keepers who lived in a house that now operates as a trampers' hut ($12), with gas cooking stove and fuel, but no cooking utensils. The hut is in a fabulous location with sea all around and views out to the Hole in the Rock, so you might want to stay more than one night.

If you'd rather not hike the length of the peninsula, engage the services of Cape Brett Walkways who offer a one-day guided walk on the outer reaches ($325) with access by cruise boat and lunch included.

Mangonui and Doubtless Bay

80km north of the Bay of Islands.
Mangonui Fish Shop, Beach Road ☎09/406 0478

The large bite out of the northern coast of Northland is **Doubtless Bay**, historically important as a provisioning stop for whaling ships. One story tells of the harbour being so choked with ships you could walk from one shore to the other. Business was transacted at the antiquated village of **Mangonui**, attractively strung along a sheltered half-kilometre of harbour with a handful of two-storey buildings with wooden verandas. Some have been preserved and operate as craft shops or cafés, but this is still very much a working village. With a lively fishing wharf and a traditional grocery perched on stilts over the water, it makes the most obvious stopping point on the way north, and has access to some excellent beaches nearby.

Several of the buses which make the trek from the Bay of Islands up to Cape Reinga, the northern tip of the North Island, stop daily at the **Mangonui Fish Shop**, which sports a great deck out over the water. It has often won awards for its excellent fish and chips and makes an excellent spot around sunset.

While ships were being restocked at Mangonui, barrels were being fixed a couple of kilometres west beside a stream crossing the strand that became known as **Coopers Beach**. This glorious and well-shaded sweep of sand is now backed by a string of motels and blighted by a rash of construction sites for big new homes. The beach is popular in January and at weekends, but at other times you might still find you have it pretty much to yourself.

Hokianga Harbour and the giant kauri

West coast of Northland, 280km north of Auckland.

The straggling mangrove-flanked **Hokianga Harbour** is the perfect antidote to Bay of Islands tourist overload. For a few days' relaxation, the tranquillity and easy pace of this rural backwater are hard to beat. It is a very traditionally Maori part of the country, but ever since the early days of the colony this is a place where Maori and Pakeha lives have intertwined.

None of the villages around the harbour amount to much, but you will probably spend most of your time on the southern shores in places like Rawene. It was here that James Clendon, a pivotal figure in the early life of the colony, lived in **Clendon House** with his half-Maori wife, Jane. Their descendants continued to live in the house until 1972.

Further west at Opononi and Omapere, the harbour's striking, deep-blue waters beautifully set off the mountainous sand dunes of North Head. Enlist the services of the local charter boat operator and you can even be taken across to the dunes and left for a few hours of **sand-boarding**.

Many people use Omapere as a staging point for visiting the Waipoua and Trounson forests, home to three-quarters of all mature **kauri trees**. Walks provide access to the most celebrated examples, notably the 1200-year-old **Tane Mahuta**, "God of the Forest", a vast wall of bark 6m wide and rising nearly 18m to the lowest branches. Only outdone for sheer bulk by the Californian sequoias, Tane Mahuta is a fabulous site, easily approached by car, but best visited at night on one of the tours run by **Footprints Waipoua** (p.30).

Trips and tours

Canyonz ℡0800/422 696, ⊛www.canyonz.co.nz. About the most fun you can have in a wetsuit around Auckland is to go canyoning, a combination of swimming, abseiling, jumping into deep pools and sliding down rock chutes. Canyonz operates in Blue Canyon ($165, 7hr) with a great variety of activities including an 8m-waterfall jump or abseil. They also offers Auckland-based day-trips down the magnificent Sleeping God canyon near Thames (Oct–May only; $225), involving descending 300m in a series of twelve drops using slides, big jumps and abseils as long as 70m (some actually through the waterfall).

Dive Tutukaka ℡0800/288 882 & 09/434 3867, ⊛www.diving.co.nz. Easily the largest operator serving the Poor Knights Islands, this very professional outfit offers two-dive day-trips ($110; including tanks $145; renting all gear $200). Snorkellers and sightseers ($90) are welcome, and everyone can use the on-board kayaks. First-time divers can try a resort dive ($250) with full gear and one-to-one instruction; a PADI open-water dive qualification will cost about $600 and take five days

Salt Air ℡0800/472 582 & 09/402 8338, ⊛www.saltair.co.nz. Plane and helicopter trips over the Bay of Islands (from $115). Also trips up to Cape Reinga ($355), landing a few kilometres short of the Cape then covering the last section by 4WD, and visiting both an east-coast beach and a west-coast beach.

Footprints Waipoua ℡09/405 8737, ⊛www.omapere.co.nz. Visit New Zealand's two largest trees – Tane Mahuta (God of the Forest) and Te Matua Ngahere (Father of the Forest) – on this leisurely four-hour Twilight Encounter Maori-led guided walk ($65). Karakia (prayers) and waiata (songs) echo through the forest as you catch the evening chorus then wander deeper, learning about use of medicinal plants and getting a real sense of Maori spirituality and their connectedness to the land. They also run a shorter Meet Tane at Night walk (1.5hr; $45) which skips the walk to Te Matua Ngahere but captures the essence of the longer visit.

Thermal Explorer

The **Thermal Explorer Highway** carves the most interesting route through the central North Island which contains more than its fair share of New Zealand's star attractions, many of them a result of its explosive geological past. Pick the highway up about an hour south of Auckland where it soon heads into the Waikato region, centred on New Zealand's fourth largest city, Hamilton, but of more interest is the surf town of **Raglan** and the limestone country around **Waitomo**.

To the southeast, the heart of the North Island is dominated by three heavyweight features: **Lake Taupo**, the country's largest; **Tongariro National Park** with its trio of active volcanoes; and the volcanic field that feeds colourful and fiercely active thermal areas, principally around **Rotorua**. If you are ticking off Kiwi icons, then time is well spent around Rotorua, where boiling mud pools plop next to spouting geysers fuelled by superheated water, which is drawn off to fill the hot pools found all over town. You'll also find the most accessible expression of Maori culture here, with highly regarded Arawa carvings and any number of groups ready to perform traditional dances and haka, and feed you fall-off-the-bone meat and juicy vegetables cooked in a hangi steam oven.

Raglan

50km west of Hamilton.

Visitors often stay far longer than they intended at the small town of **Raglan**, which hugs the south side of the large and picturesque Raglan Harbour. This long-standing weekend destination is seeing a renaissance, gaining permanent residents drawn by the town's bohemian arts-and-crafts tenor and the laid-back spirit of the surf community. Raglan's Manu Bay and Whale Bay have an international reputation among surfers as some of the best left-handed breaks in the world.

Indeed, Raglan is New Zealand's only real **surfing destination**, with board-topped old cars parked outside the surf shops and a lot of sun-bleached hair and baggy pants in the cafés. **Surf lessons** are available (see p.36) and there are a couple of backpacker places.

Almost everything of note lines **Bow Street**, its central row of Phoenix palms shading banks, several good restaurants and a selection of craft shops. At the street's western end it butts up against the sparkling harbour, where a footbridge provides access to the main campsite and a safe swimming beach. About the only specific sight is the **Raglan Museum**, in an old police station (Sat & Sun 1–3.30pm; donation), which has a modest local history collection, both European and Maori.

Waitomo walks

Waitomo Caves, 75km south of Hamilton. Ruakuri Caves.

The caves at **Waitomo** are famed for their adrenalin-pumping trips, where you can enjoy long abseils, and float on tyre tubes through the darkness with thousands of glow-worms above.

If this isn't your idea of fun, go for the **Ruakuri Natu-**

ral Tunnel track (2km return; 45min), surely one of the most delightful short walks in the country. It starts 3km west of the visitor centre, and follows the Waitomo Stream on boardwalks past cave entrances. Ducking and weaving through short tunnel sections, you eventually reach a huge cave where the stream temporarily threads underground. It is especially magical at night when glow-worms light the bush on the banks.

There's more free stuff 20km further west at the **Mangapohue Natural Bridge**, where an easy fifteen-minute loop trail winds through forest. A riverside boardwalk leads into a delightful, narrow limestone gorge topped by a remarkable natural double bridge formed by the remains of a collapsed cave roof. Dramatic at any time, it is especially picturesque at night when the underside of the bridges glimmer with myriad glow-worms.

Maungatautari Ecological Island

35km southeast of Hamilton. Maungatautari Ecological Island Trust
Ⓦ www.maungatrust.org.

You'll read elsewhere in this book about wildlife sanctuaries either on offshore islands or on the mainland ringed by predator-proof fence. Two things make **Maungatautari** special. The first is its scale. When complete the 47km fence will enclose 3400 hectares – the whole extinct volcano and its forested flanks. Perhaps more significantly it is a community project which is currently a little over halfway through raising the $14 million needed. Accordingly the fence is only half built, but with pest-trapping and baiting well established, the benefits are already being experienced. The morning chorus is coming back and will soon be boosted by the calls of several of New Zealand's endangered bird species.

The public have unrestricted access to this "mainland island" using specially designed double gates.

Waimangu Thermal Valley

20km south of Rotorua. Daily 8.30am–5pm; walking tour $28, boat cruise $35 Ⓦ www.waimangu.co.nz.

At the southern limit of the volcanic rift blown out by Mount Tarawera lies **Waimangu Thermal Valley**. Among the world's youngest thermal areas, this is also New Zealand's largest and most lushly vegetated.

A streamside path cuts through a valley choked with scrub and native bush that has re-established itself since the 1886 Tarawera eruption. The regeneration process has been periodically interrupted by smaller eruptions, including one in 1917 that created the 100m-diameter **Frying Pan Lake**, the world's largest hot spring. Impressive quantities of hot water welling up from the depths is the attraction of the **Inferno Crater**, an inverted cone where mesmerizing steam patterns partly obscure the powder-blue water. The water level rises and falls according to a rigid 38-day cycle – filling to the rim for 21 days, overflowing for two days then gradually falling to 8m below the rim over the next fifteen days. More run-of-the-mill steaming pools and hissing vents line the stream, which also passes the muddy depression where, from 1900 to 1904, the **Waimangu Geyser** regularly spouted water to an astonishing height of 400m, carrying rocks and black mud with it.

The path through the valley ends at the wharf on the shores of Lake Rotomahana, where the rust-red sides of Mount Tarawera dominate the far horizon. From here, frequent free shuttle buses run back up the road to the visitor centre and gentle, commentated, 45-minute cruises chug around the lake past steaming cliffs, fumaroles and over the site of the Pink and White Terraces.

Whirinaki Forest Park

Near Murupara, 80km southeast of Rotorua.

State Highway 38 runs southeast from Rotorua bound for Lake Waikaremoana, two tortuous and winding hours away. But if it is wilderness you are after it is far easier to stop at the easily accessible **Whirinaki Forest Park**, a wild and wonderful slice of country that harbours some of the densest and most impressive stands of bush on the North Island: native pines on the river flats, and beech on the steep volcanic uplands between them.

Both ecosystems support a wonderfully rich **birdlife** with tui, bellbirds, parakeets and even the rare brownish-red kaka. The forest is now protected from the loggers' chainsaw, after a close shave in the late 1970s and early 1980s, when it saw one of the country's fiercest and most celebrated **environmental battles**. In early 1978, protesters had succeeded in preventing logging by occupying trees in the Pureora State Forest to the west of Lake Taupo. Anticipating similar action at Whirinaki and fearing for their livelihood, the local Ngati Whare people blockaded the road into the forest; conflict was only avoided through intense negotiation. By 1987 logging of all native timber had ceased (except for totara cut for ceremonial-carving purposes) and the mill had closed.

In a few hours you can sample some of the best of the Whirinaki Forest Park along the **Whirinaki Track** which visits the churning Te Whaiti-nui-a-tio Canyon and **Whirinaki Falls**, where the Whirinaki River cascades over an old lava flow. The full **Whirinaki Track** (27km; 2 days) penetrates deeper into the forest. **Whirinaki Guided Walks Ltd** provides single and multi-day walks and marae experiences (including overnight stays for groups). This walk programme offers cultural components, including on-track interpretation by Maori guides whose ancestors have used the forest for food and medicine for centuries – practices which are still maintained today.

Lake Taupo

Central North Island.

Lake Taupo is New Zealand's largest lake, 30km across and created by a massive cataclysm in 186AD. No one was around in New Zealand to report such an exact date, but the explosion was so enormous that Chinese scholars reported darkening of the skies and the Romans described the heavens turning blood-red. Altogether the volcano spewed out 24 cubic kilometres of rock, debris and ash, more than ten times the amount produced by the Krakatoa and Mount St Helens eruptions combined.

The gigantic crater collapsed and has since been filled with Lake Taupo. Thousands come every year to **skydive** around its shores, fire golf balls into it in the hope of hitting a moored floating golf platform, and fish for trout. Some of the best fun can be had simply cruising its waters, best done by kayak (see below). One of the most appealing easy destinations is Mine Bay, where a ten-metre rock face is covered with modern Maori **rock carvings**. Dating from the late 1970s, they depict a stylized image of a man's face heavy with *moko* (tattoos), together with *tuatara* (lizard-like reptiles) and female forms draped over nearby rocks.

Trips and tours

Raglan Surfing School ☎07/825 7873, ⊛www.raglansurfingschool .co.nz. Surf lessons (from 3hr; $79) using a specially made soft board including all gear and transport. There are longer packages if you get the bug.

Taupo Tandem Skydiving ☎07/377 0428, ⊛www.taupotandemskydiving .com. The biggest of Taupo's skydiving operators offering highly competitive tandem jumps from 12,000 feet ($145) and 15,000 feet ($229), with fabulous views of Lake Taupo.

Wilderness Escapes ☎07/378 3413, ⊛www.wildernessescapes.co.nz. Highly professional guided adventure trips around the central North Island, perhaps best for guided kayaking trips on Lake Taupo. Visit the Mine Bay rock carvings (half-day; $85) or venture further afield on full day-trips ($210) and overnight adventures.

Pacific Coast Highway

The long sweep of coast east from Auckland around to Hawke's Bay is followed by the **Pacific Coast Highway**, an ideal route for beach lovers and those keen for a bit of seclusion. It includes some of the most popular summer-holiday destinations on the North Island as well as one of the least-visited parts of the country.

The long and jagged **Coromandel Peninsula** is blessed with some of the country's best sandy beaches and a gorgeous climate. Specific sights aren't numerous, but Driving Creek Railway is definitely worth riding. The gorgeous beaches continue east around the **Bay of Plenty** which finishes with a flourish at the volcanic **White Island**. You can raft the wild and remote **Motu River**, which reaches the sea on the **East Cape**, a sparsely populated area with a dramatic coastline and slow pace of life. The pace picks up in Hawke's Bay, where interest focuses on touring the beautiful **wine country** while based in Napier. This is one of New Zealand's nicest provincial capitals, not least because of its small-scale **Art Deco** buildings.

White Island

50km north of Whakatane; access by boat trips with White Island Tours ☎0800/733 529 & 07/308 9588, ⓦwww.whiteisland.co.nz; full-day tours daily all year; $150.

The occasionally rough boat trip doesn't seem to deter a

steady stream of visitors to **White Island** (Whaakari) with its other-worldly towers of gas, steam and ash, spewing from a crater lake 60m below sea level.

The ongoing clash of the Indo-Australian and Pacific plates has resulted in the upwards thrust of super-heated rock through the ocean floor creating a massive **volcanic** structure. **Sulphur**, for use in fertilizer manufacture, was sporadically mined on the island from the 1880s, but all enterprises were plagued by catastrophic eruptions, landslides and economic misfortune. The island was abandoned in 1934, and these days is home only to 60,000 grey-faced **petrels** and 10,000 **gannets**.

Tours begin at the 1923 sulphur-processing factory, gradually being eaten away by the high sulphur content of the atmosphere, and progress to an open-sided crater where you stand in the clouds with a gas mask on. Amid pools of bubbling mud and pillars of smoke and steam, you get the chance to see fumaroles surrounded by bright yellow and white crystal deposits that re-form daily in new and bizarre shapes.

The crystal-clear and abundant waters around the island make this one of the best **dive spots** in New Zealand (see p.44).

Rafting the Motu River

Raukumara Ranges, east of Whakatane.

Some of the best **wilderness rafting** trips in New Zealand are on the Grade III–IV **Motu River**, which is hidden deep in the mountain terrain of the remote Raukumara Ranges, with long stretches of white water plunging through gorges and valleys to the Bay of Plenty coast. In 1981, after a protracted campaign against hydro-dam builders, the Motu became New Zealand's first designated "wild and scenic" river. Access by 4WD, helicopter and jetboat makes one- and two-day trips possible, but to capture the essence of this remote region you should consider one of the longer trips on which you'll see no sign of civilization for three days – a magical and eerie experience.

Currently, the only company running regular trips is Rotorua-based **Wet'n'Wild Rafting** (℡0800/462 723, ⓦwww.wetnwildrafting.co.nz), who offer trips ranging from two-day outings (with helicopter access $750), to the full four-day adventure (without helicopter access $690) from the headwaters to the sea.

Driving the East Cape

A 330km loop around the northeastern tip of the North Island.

The East Cape, the nub of land jutting into the South Pacific northeast of Opotiki and Gisborne, is one of the most sparsely populated areas in New Zealand. The Pacific Coast Highway (SH35) hugs the rugged coastline much of the way, providing spectacular sea views on a fine day.

As soon as you enter the region you'll notice a change of pace, epitomized by the occasional sight of a lone horseback rider clopping along the road. **Maori** make up a significant percentage of the East Coast's population, and draw on their strong culture to cope with the hardships of this untamed landscape and uncertain economic prospects. Over eighty percent of land tenure here is in Maori hands, something that sits well with the people: most feel in greater control of their destiny than Maori do elsewhere.

The **coast** is very much the focus, and whatever time isn't spent gazing out of the vehicle window is likely to be enjoyed on the beach or in the water. That said, there are hiking opportunities, and just about everywhere someone will be happy to take you **horse trekking**, either along the beach or into the bush. In general, the **towns**, such as they are, don't have much to recommend them, though at weekends you might like to find a pub if you fancy a country-music jukebox singalong. One place of note is the seaside hamlet of

Whangara, star of the movie *Whale Rider* (see p.44).

The few genuine highlights in the region include the picture-perfect, white clapboard Anglican church at **Ruakokore**, standing on a promontory framed by the blue ocean; the lighthouse at **East Cape**; and the country's longest wharf, the 660m-long jetty at **Tolaga Bay**.

Lake Waikaremoana

90km north of Napier.

The magnificent, bush-girt **Lake Waikaremoana** fills a huge scalloped bowl at an altitude of over 585m. The lake came into being around 2200 years ago when a huge bank of sandstone boulders was dislodged from the Ngamoko range, blocking the river that once drained the valleys and thereby forming the lake. Maori have a more poetic explanation of the lake's creation, pointing to the work of Hau-Mapuhia, the recalcitrant daughter of Mahu, who was drowned by her father and turned into a *taniwha*, or "water spirit". In a frenzied effort to get to the sea, she charged in every direction, thereby creating the various arms of the lake. As she frantically ran south towards Onepoto, the dawn caught her, turning her to stone at a spot where the lake is said to ripple from time to time, in a watery memory of her titanic struggle.

One of the beauties of the lake is that there is no town nearby, just a visitor centre and a motor camp, both well set-up for helping hikers tackle the four-day **Lake Waikaremoana Track**, one of New Zealand's designated "Great Walks".

Art Deco Napier

If the dark cloud of the 1931 earthquake had a silver lining, it was the chance for **Napier** to rebuild from scratch. In the spirit of the times, almost everything was designed according to the precepts of the **Art Deco** movement, giving Napier a rare stylistic uniformity. It ranks alongside Miami Beach as having one of the largest collections of Art Deco buildings in the world.

Architects adopted fountains (a symbol of renewal), sunbursts, chevrons, lightning flashes and stylized fluting to embellish the highly formalized but asymmetric designs. After years of neglect, this legacy was seen with fresh eyes in the mid-1980s when the **Art Deco Trust** began preserving buildings and providing funding for shopkeepers to pick out distinctive architectural detail in original pastel colours.

Visitors with only a passing interest in architecture can get a sense of what the fuss is about by wandering along the half-dozen streets in the city centre, notably **Emerson Street**, with its particularly homogeneous run of upper-floor frontages. Worth special attention here is the **ASB Bank**, on the corner of Hastings Street, its exterior adorned with fern shoots and a mask from the head of a *taiaha* (a long fighting club), while its interior has a fine Maori rafter design. On Tennyson Street, look for the flamboyant **Daily Telegraph** building with stylized fountains capping the pilasters, and the **Municipal Theatre**, built in the late 1930s in a strikingly geometric and streamlined form.

Just outside the centre in the port suburb of Ahuriri, the **National Tobacco Company Building** is the single most frequently used image of Deco Napier and exhibits a decorative richness seldom seen on industrial buildings. All things Deco are celebrated during the annual **Art Deco Weekend** in February (see p.93).

Hawke's Bay wine country

Around the two small cities of Napier and Hastings.

Napier and Hastings are almost entirely encircled by the **Hawke's Bay's wine country**, one of New Zealand's largest and most exalted viticultural regions. Hawke's Bay produces fine **Chardonnay** and **Cabernet Sauvignon**, and as scientific studies unravel the complexity of the local soils and microclimates, growers have begun to diversify into **Merlot** and **Sauvignon Blanc**.

Vines were first planted here in 1851 by French Marist missionaries, ostensibly to produce sacramental wine. The excess was sold, and the commercial aspect of the operation continues today as the Mission Estate Winery. Some fifty-odd years later, newer wineries favoured the fertile plains, but as tastes became more sophisticated such sites were forsaken for the river terraces such as these along **Gimblett Road**. These retain the day's heat, are free from moist sea breezes and are producing increasingly praiseworthy wines.

The **Hawke's Bay wine trail** threads through it all, past forty-odd wineries, most offering free tastings. Many places are now fashioning themselves as "destination wineries" where tasting is almost an adjunct to admiring the architecture, lunching at one of the vineyard restaurants, enjoying a picnic in the landscaped grounds, or maybe

Epicurean Hawke's Bay

Hawke's Bay is New Zealand's longest established wine region, and good wine should always be served with good food. Many of the vineyards have impressive **restaurants**, while others have gone out of their way to create gorgeous spots for picnics. Arm yourself with the region's free wine and food leaflets and go wild, sampling everything from freshly pressed olive oil to wonderful cheeses and exotic chocolates.

If you'd rather find what you need in one place, make for the vibrant **farmers' markets**. The best is probably the **Hawke's Bay Farmers Market'** (Sun 8.30am–12.30pm), held at the Hawke's Bay Showgrounds in Hastings, but Napier's equivalent (Sat from 8.30am) is perhaps more convenient, right downtown.

looking at a small museum.

If you have your own transport, head out with a copy of the free *A Guide to the Wineries* leaflet. If you can't find an abstemious driver, take a **wine tour** (see p.44) most of which visit four or five wineries over the course of a morning or afternoon.

Whitianga and Hot Water Beach

East Coast, Coromandel Peninsula.

Attractive **Whitianga** clusters where the estuarine Whitianga Harbour meets the broad sweep of **Mercury Bay**. This huge bite out of the Coromandel Peninsula coastline was named by Captain Cook who stopped here in 1769 so that his party of scientists could observe Mercury pass across the face of the sun.

Whitianga makes a good base from which to make a series of half-day and **day-trips** to some wonderfully secluded spots, so allow a couple of days here. Just across the narrow harbour mouth and strung along Mercury Bay's eastern shore are several unusual beaches, reached by passenger ferry to **Ferry Landing**, from where you can catch a bus or strike out along scenic coastal tracks. The area is also served by roads branching off the southbound SH25, which loops around the deeply indented harbour. Two gems here are **Cathedral Cove**, a stunning geological formation, and **Hot Water Beach**, renowned for its natural hot-water springs bubbling beneath the sand. Bordering part of the eastern shore is **Cathedral Cove Marine Reserve**, whose protected waters are a great spot for snorkelling and scuba diving.

Trips and tours

Bay Carving ☎ 07/866 4021, Ⓦ www.dreamland.co.nz/baycarving. Create your own bone carving in a couple of hours using your own design or one of assorted traditional Maori and contemporary designs.

Dive White Island ☎ 0800/348 394, Ⓦ www.divewhite.co.nz. Excellent dive trips to the waters off White Island – visibility is commonly around 20m. Two dive-days cost from $190 with your own gear to $260 for full rental and $395 for a one-to-one beginner's dive with an instructor. They'll also take you snorkelling on a sightseeing trip (full day, $150 including lunch).

Grape Escape ☎ 06/879 8735, Ⓦ www.grapeescapenz.co.nz. Half-day trips of the Hawke's Bay wineries ($45) are available but their speciality is full-day gourmet tours ($115) also visiting food producers, farmers' markets and including a picnic lunch platter.

Kiwi Dundee Adventures ☎ 07/865 8809, Ⓦ www.kiwidundee.co.nz. Very popular eco-tours into the native forest of the Coromandel Peninsula and further afield, led by the idiosyncratic and entertaining Doug Johansen, who goes by the title "Kiwi Dundee". Everything from day walks to five-day treks around parts of the North Island.

On Yer Bike ☎ 06/879 8735, Ⓦ www.onyerbikehb.co.nz. Cycle around the Hawke's Bay vineyards using easy itineraries ranging from two wineries in 14km to six in 23km. All-day bike rental (tandems available), route map, emergency mobile phone and a packed lunch are included in the $50 fee.

Walking Legends ☎ 07/345 7363, Ⓦ www.walkinglegends.com. Small-group four-day all-inclusive guided walks ($890) around Lake Waikaremoana with engaging and informative guides. Plenty of great views, and fishing on the first two days.

Whale Rider Tours ☎ 06/868 6139. Entertaining tours (Mon, Wed & Fri 10am–2pm; $50; minimum 4) around the tiny settlement where much of *Whale Rider* was shot. You'll be instructed to meet at tiny Whangara, 30km north of Gisborne, where the Taumaunu family will show you around a working *marae* and relate Maori legends including that of the Whale Rider, Paikea.

Western North Island

Much of the **Western North Island** is well off the main tourist arteries, and all the better for it. It is an area best absorbed slowly; spend an afternoon in a timewarped fishing community or drive slowly along almost forgotten highways, sampling their small-time charms and meeting the locals.

Geographically the region is dominated by the giant thumb-print peninsula of **Taranaki** ranged around the symmetrical cone of **Mount Taranaki** (2518m). The mountain is the focal point for some great hiking, specifically the slog to the snowcapped summit. The northern slopes run down to Taranaki's biggest town, **New Plymouth**, with its contemporary art showcase the **Govett-Brewster Art Gallery**.

Inland, the **Forgotten World Highway** links Taranaki with the Whanganui River, its waters best explored by canoe or jetboat, both of which give access to the curious **Bridge to Nowhere**. Drivers can weave south along the Whanganui's lower reaches following the **Whanganui River Road** and back to the coast at Wanganui, or stay inland and head for River Valley.

Govett-Brewster Art Gallery

Cnr Queen Street and King Street, New Plymouth
Ⓦ www.govettbrewster.org.nz; daily 10.30am–5pm; free.

The **Govett-Brewster** is one of New Zealand's foremost contemporary art galleries, with ever-changing and challenging exhibitions. It is home to the Len Lye Foundation, which owns a huge permanent collection of works by New Zealand-born sculptor, film-maker and conceptual artist **Len Lye** (1901–80), who designed the iconic Wind Wand that sways mesmerizingly on the New Plymouth waterfront.

Lye developed a fascination with movement in early experiments in kinetic sculpture and animated "cameraless" films, which he painstakingly stencilled on the actual film. After World War II he exploited the flexibility of stainless-steel rods, loops and strips to create abstract "tangible motion sculptures". The erratic movements of these motor-driven sculptures give them an air of anarchy, which is most evident in his best-known work, 1977's Trilogy – more commonly referred to as Flip and Two Twisters – three motorized metal sheets that wildly shake and contort until winding down to a final convulsion. Lye envisaged his works as being monumental and set outdoors, but was always aware of the technical limitations of his era and considered his projects to be works of the twenty-first century. The Wind Wand is the most visible and largest yet, though the foundation has also been instrumental in creating Lye's Water Whirler on the Wellington waterfront.

The gallery usually only has a small amount of Lye's work on display at any one time, but you can always watch some of his films and a documentary on his life and work; if none are showing, just ask.

Hiking Mount Taranaki

The province of Taranaki is dominated by the conical, snowcapped 2518-metre **Mount Taranaki**, a dormant volcano whose profile compares favourably with Japan's Mount Fuji. The mountain is the focal point for **Egmont National Park**, the boundary of which forms an arc with a ten-kilometre radius around the mountain. Farmland lies all about, but within the national park the mountain's lower slopes are cloaked in native bush, which gradually changes to stunted flag-form trees, lopsidedly shaped by the constant buffeting of the wind higher up. Higher still, vegetation gives way to loose scoria slopes, hard work for those hiking to the summit.

The most popular hike is up the Northern Route to the **summit** (10km return; 6–8hr; 1560m ascent) from the North Egmont visitor centre. Even during the **summer hiking season** (Jan to mid-April) bad weather sweeps in frighteningly quickly, and hikers should seek advice on conditions at the visitor centre, and follow it.

A safer bet is the **Pouakai Circuit** (25km loop; 2 days) which turns its back on the big mountain and heads north around the lower Pouakai Range, from where the views of Taranaki can be wonderful.

The Forgotten World Highway

State Hwy 43 from Taumarunui southwest to Stratford in Taranaki.

For a taste of genuinely rural New Zealand it's hard to beat the **Forgotten World Highway**, a rugged 155-kilometre road that twists through the hills west of Taumarunui. It takes a minimum of three hours, but a lot longer if you want to explore the thirty-odd points of historic and geographical interest along the way. The road is particularly well suited to those in campervans who will find numerous places to park up overnight.

The road snakes through the sedimentary limestone of the **Tangarakau Gorge**, the highlight of the trip, with steep bush-draped cliffs rising up above the river. At the entrance to the gorge, a small sign directs you along a short trail to the picturesque site of **Joshua Morgan's grave**, the final resting place of an early surveyor. At the crest of a ridge you pass through the dark **Moki Tunnel**, then steadily descend to the village of **Whangamomona**. It only has around thirty residents, but on October 28, 1989, it declared itself a republic after the government altered the provincial boundaries, taking it out of Taranaki. The declaration is celebrated in January every odd-numbered year (Jan 20 in 2007), with the swearing in of the president, whip-cracking, gumboot-throwing competitions, and a good deal of drinking and eating, all shared by hordes who come to witness and partake; a special train even runs from Auckland and Hamilton.

Celebrations revolve around the 1911 Whangamomona Hotel (℡06/762 5823, ℮whangamomonahotel@clear.net.nz), where you can get your passport stamped or buy a Whangamomonian version ($3), while wetting your whistle. The hotel serves dinner and offers bed and breakfast.

Bridge to Nowhere

Whanganui National Park. Only accessible by jetboat, kayak or a long walk. Several companies provide access, including Bridge to Nowhere Tours and Waka Tours (see p.51).

Vincent Ward's recent film *River Queen* starred Samantha Morton as a woman torn between Pakeha and Maori worlds during the New Zealand Wars of the 1860s. It was set along the Whanganui River which winds through the **Whanganui National Park**, a land virtually without roads. Access is either by jetboat, or by canoeing the **Whanganui River Journey**, a popular three- to five-day canoe trip staying in huts and campsites along the riverbank.

▼ Pack Horse crayfish, White Island

TAUMATAWHAKATANGI
HANGAKOAUAUOTAMATEA
TURIPUKAKAPIKIMAUNGA
HORONUKUPOKAIWHEN
UAKITANATAHU

THE PLACE WHERE TAMATEA, THE MAN WITH
THE BIG KNEES, WHO SLID, CLIMBED, AND
SWALLOWED MOUNTAINS, KNOWN AS LANDEATER,
PLAYED HIS FLUTE TO HIS LOVED ONE.

Guinness Book of R.

▲ The longest place name in the
world, Hawkes Bay

▼ Walking on White Island

▲ Collecting shellfish

▲ Horse trek, Glenorchy

BE A REAL FREEWHEELER.

Don't be a tourist, be an explorer.

With our newly transformed long-haul cabins, your adventure starts the moment you take off.

Once you arrive, only Air New Zealand can fly you to 25 destinations across New Zealand. So you can get further off the beaten track and try anything from canyoning at Wanaka to rafting along the Motu River.

To discover more of New Zealand, and find our best fares, book online at airnewzealand.co.uk

AIR NEW ZEALAND
Bringing New Zealand closer.

▲ Refreshment stop on
the Copland Track

▼ Rafting on the Rangitata River

▲ Whangapoua, Coromandel

▲ Swing bridge, Stewart Island

One of the highlights of the journey is the **Bridge to Nowhere**, a big concrete road bridge over a deep gorge but with no roads leading to or from it. It was the product of European attempts to stamp their mark on this wild landscape. In 1917, the surrounding Mangapurua Valley was opened up for settlement by servicemen returning from World War I, who little realized they were trading one battlefield for another. Plagued by economic hardship, remoteness and difficulty of access, many had abandoned their farms by the 1930s. In an attempt to rejuvenate the area the authorities constructed the bridge in 1936, but after a major flood in 1942 it was cut off, the three remaining families ordered out, and the valley officially closed. Today, the only other signs of habitation are old fence lines, stands of exotic trees planted by the farmers and occasional brick chimneys.

Whanganui River Road and Jerusalem

Runs between Raetihi and Wanganui, west of State Hwy 4.

Canoe and jetboat trips navigate the main body of the **Whanganui National Park**, but there are outlying sections to the south which can be accessed along the partly unsealed **Whanganui River Road**.

Hugging the river's left bank, the twisting River Road forms the supply route for the four hundred people or so who live along it, but offers no shops, pubs or petrol stations, and only a handful of places to stay.

It is all about the journey rather than specific sights, though you should stop at *Hiruharama* (Maori for Jerusalem), originally a Maori village and Catholic mission which in the 1970s was briefly and infamous "free love" commune led by celebrated Kiwi poet **James K. Baxter**. The only real settlement of note in these parts is **Koriniti** (Maori for Corinth), home to a lovely small church and a trio of traditional Maori buildings, the best being a 1920s meeting house, all down a side road. You can enter the church, but it is a fairly private community and the rest is best viewed from the road.

Undoubtedly the best **place to stay** around here is the **Flying Fox** (see opposite) which can only be reached by a wire-suspended cart which is hauled across the river. If you don't fancy the drive, consider joining the **Rural Mail Coach Tour** trips (see opposite).

Adventures at River Valley

Central North Island, 30km east of Taihape. ☎06/388 1444, ⓦwww.rivervalley.co.nz.

Driving south of Tongariro National Park along State Highway 1, most people weave through the Rangitikei hill country without stopping. Few realize the fun to be had at River Valley at the end of a side road on the banks of the wild Rangitikei River. Many come to experience some of the best **whitewater rafting** ($129) in the country on the gorge section of the Rangitikei. Ten major Grade IV and Grade V rapids are packed into this beautiful twelve-kilometre run. Further downstream there's scenic **eco-rafting** ($129) and lovely horse trekking around ($69 for 2hr).

River Valley also work with nearby Mokai Gravity Canyon, who operate a 80m bungy jump ($125) and a 1km-long flying fox ($99). **Accommodation** ranges from camping and backpacker dorms to the modest luxury of en-suite rooms and cabins.

Trips and tours

Bridge to Nowhere Tours
ⓣ 0800/480 308,
ⓦ www.bridgetonowheretours.co.nz.
Major operator offering a five-hour
combination trip to the Bridge to
Nowhere ($90) jetboating upstream
and canoeing back down. Other jetboat
and canoe options, plus a riverside
lodge.

The Flying Fox ⓣ 06/342 8160,
ⓦ www.theflyingfox.co.nz. A
wonderfully relaxing romantic
hideaway only accessible by boat
or aerial cableway: prior booking is
essential. An eclectic range of found
objects and scavenged pieces of old
buildings have been imaginatively
combined to create self-contained
"cottages". Wood-fired bush baths and
solar-heated showers add to the appeal
and the fascinating range of books,
old vinyl and CDs should keep you
entertained for days. Choose from self-
catering cabins ($70–110) or camping
($15). Predominantly organic slow-food
meals can be provided, or bring your
own food.

Rural Mail Coach Tour ⓣ 06/347
7534, ⓦ www.whanganuitours.co.nz.
A genuine mail delivery service which
doubles as a tour, stopping frequently
at houses along the way as well as
points of interest. You may be able to
take a jetboat trip up to the Bridge to
Nowhere and still meet the minibus
for the return journey. Mon–Fri
7.30am; $35.

Waka Tours ⓣ 06/385 4811,
ⓦ www.wakatours.net. Excellent
three-day guided canoe tours ($560)
on the scenic middle reaches of the
Whanganui River, learning about
the river environment from a Maori
perspective, taking bush walks and
staying in *marae*, where you're given
a traditional welcome. A true cultural
exchange.

Lower North Island

The North Island finishes with a flourish at **Wellington**, New Zealand's capital city, and with around 400,000 residents its second most populous. Strung across steep hills, wedged between the glistening waters of **Wellington Harbour** and the turbulent seas of Cook Strait, Wellington is arguably New Zealand's most attractive large city. As the principal departure point for ferries **crossing Cook Strait** to the South Island it is sometimes only afforded a fleeting glimpse, but it makes a great base for exploring the region.

Most southbound traffic approaches Wellington along the western Kapiti Coast commuter belt where you should definitely pay a visit to **Kapiti Island**. The main alternative is through the **Wairarapa** region where the **Pukaha Mount Bruce National Wildlife Centre** gives unparalleled opportunities to see native bird conservation at close quarters. There are more traditional sybaritic charms further south in the compact wine region around **Martinborough**, and if you like your hiking at the easy end of the spectrum with hot showers and good food then consider booking yourself and some friends on the **Tora Coastal Walk**.

Pukaha Mount Bruce National Wildlife Centre

50km north of Masterton ☎06/375 8004,
ⓦwww.mtbruce.org.nz; daily 9am–4.30pm; $8.

Encircled by majestic forest, the **Pukaha Mount Bruce National Wildlife Centre** is one of the best places in the country to view endangered native birds; indeed, it is a pioneer in the field of captive-breeding programmes. Visitors have the chance to see some of the world's rarest birds – kokako, kakariki, Campbell Island teal, hihi, kiwi and takahe – in spacious aviaries set along a one-kilometre trail through lowland primeval forest. Beyond the trail several thousand hectares of forest are used for reintroducing birds to the wild. The generous size of the cages on the trail and the thick foliage often make the creatures hard to spot, so you'll need to be patient (Jan & Feb are the best times); more immediate gratification comes in the form of a stand of Californian redwoods, a nocturnal kiwi house, reptilian tuatara and a closed-circuit camera trained on the birds' nests in the breeding season (Oct–March). A twenty-minute audiovisual in the visitor centre gives a moving account of the decline of birdlife in New Zealand; eels are fed at 1.30pm, while at 3pm each day a flock of kaka come to feed. The centre relies heavily on donations, so give if you can.

Martinborough

35km south of Masterton and 85km east of Wellington.

Over the last twenty years, tiny **Martinborough** has been transformed from an obscure farming town into the centre of a compact wine region, synonymous with some of New Zealand's finest red wines. Weekends see the arrival of the Wellington smart set to lunch at the appealing cafés and

Private walks: the third way

Kiwi trekkers have always been used to rugged tracks and spartan **backcountry** huts. Such hardship is valued by traditionalists who scorn the broad, smooth-surfaced tracks and relatively sophisticated huts of the designated **Great Walks**, which are largely the preserve of foreign tourists. Both styles of tramping are undertaken in publicly owned National Parks and forests where the tramping is free (though the huts are not).

Now there's a third way. A growing band of private landowners (often farmers but sometimes community groups) are opening up previously inaccessible land to walkers. The emphasis is usually on relatively short days of easy-to-moderate walking with a comfortable cabin or lodge at the end of the day. Your bags can often be delivered to the door (so you only need carry a day pack), hot showers sometimes feature, and there's often a fridge stocked with food and the option of having your meal cooked for you.

The first such walk was the Banks Peninsula Track, opened in the late 1980s, but now there are a couple of dozen including the **Tora Coastal Walk**, and the **Kaikoura Coastal Walk** in the Coastal Otago/Southland region.

restaurants and load up their shiny 4WDs at the two-dozen **wineries** that are within a kilometre or so of town. On Mondays and Tuesdays much of the town simply shuts down to recover.

The region's first vintage was in 1984 when four wineries – Ata Rangi, Dry River, Chifney and Martinborough – reinvented Martinborough as the North Island's coolest and driest of grape-growing region, specializing in outstanding Pinot Noir, very good Cabernet Sauvignon and crisp and aromatic Riesling. Best of all, many of the wineries are within walking distance of town, and a day's tasting doesn't have to involve sacrifices on the part of the driver. If you'd rather not venture out of town at all, the wineries bring their produce to you at **Martinborough Wine Centre**, 6 Kitchener St (ⓦwww.martinboroughwinecentre.co.nz), where you can taste a variety of local wines ($1.50–2.50 per taste).

Martinborough is no slouch at promoting its viticultural prowess, and the best time to visit is during one of its **festivals**. The exclusive Toast Martinborough (third Sun in Nov) is usually sold out far in advance, but try to get along to one of the **Martinborough Fairs** (first Sat in Feb & March; ⓦwww.martinboroughfair.org.nz), huge country fêtes during which the streets radiating from the central square are lined with stalls selling arts and crafts.

Karori Wildlife Sanctuary

3km west of downtown Wellington ☎04/920 9213,
ⓦwww.sanctuary.org.nz; daily 10am–5pm; $8.

The **Karori Wildlife Sanctuary** is an ambitious project to restore a sliver of New Zealand native bush (and attendant wildlife) to 253 hectares of urban Wellington. Designed around two century-old reservoirs which formerly supplied Wellington's drinking water, the managing trust first designed and constructed an 8.6km-long **predator-proof fence** which is intended to keep out all introduced mammals. As well as restocking the area with native trees and eradicating weeds, the trust is introducing endangered birds. Along the 35km of paths you might see weka, saddleback, kaka, tuatara, morepork, tui, bellbird, whitehead and North Island robins. You'll also understand why early European arrivals to New Zealand were so impressed with the birdsong.

It's fun spending half a day exploring by yourself, but worthwhile joining a two-hour **guided tour** ($40). Alternatively, try one of the wonderful night tours ($45), starting just after sunset and giving you a chance to hear (and maybe see) kiwi.

Crossing Cook Strait

Interislander ⓣ0800/802 802, ⓦwww.interislander.co.nz, and Blue Bridge ⓣ0800/844 844, ⓦwww.bluebridge.co.nz; a little over 3hr.

Crossing Cook Strait, between the two main islands, is often seen as a chore, but should really be approached as a short cruise. The views of Wellington as you glide out of the harbour are magical, especially if you get an early morning departure or leave as the city lights start peppering the growing dusk. Cook Strait itself is often rough, but relief is at hand as you enter the **Marlborough Sounds**, specifically Tory Channel, which is only a few hundred metres wide. After assorted twists and turns the channel opens out into beautiful Queen Charlotte Sound for the last half hour to Picton.

Tora Coastal Walk

Wairarapa, 35km south of Martinborough. ⓣ06/307 8862, ⓦwww.toracoastalwalk.co.nz. Operates Oct–April. $160.

Relaxed and very enjoyable private walk that completes a three-day, three-night loop in southern Wairarapa. It's a harmonious combination of wild coastal walking, pretty farmland, open ridges and native bush with accommodation in fully equipped farm cottages. There's plenty of time for beachcombing or watching the seals, and at the end of the day there's a hot shower and meals cooked for you (at extra cost).

Kapiti Island

50km north of Wellington. Compulsory landing permits ($9) available from the Department of Conservation. Daily boat access with Kapiti Tours ⓣ0800/527 484, ⓦwww.kapititours.co.nz ($35).

One of the few easily accessible island **nature reserves** in New Zealand, 10km by 2km **Kapiti Island**, is a magical spot, its bush, once cleared for farmland, now home to birdlife that has become rare or extinct on the mainland. In 1822, infamous Maori chief **Te Rauparaha** captured the island from its first known Maori inhabitants and, with his people the Ngati Toa, used it as a base until his death in 1849; it's thought that he may be buried somewhere on the island, but the site of his grave is unknown. For this, and other reasons, the island is considered extremely spiritual to Maori, and was designated a reserve in 1897.

Late January and February are the best months to visit, when the **birdlife** is at its most active, but at any time of the year you're likely to see kaka (bush parrots that may alight on your head or shoulder), weka, kakariki (parakeets), whiteheads (bush canaries), tui, bellbirds, fantails, wood pigeons, robins and a handful of the 250 takahe that exist in the world. The island can be explored on two fairly steep **walking tracks** – the Trig Track and the Wilkinson Track – which effectively form a loop by meeting near the island's highest point, Tuteremoana (521m). There are spectacular views from the summit, though the widest variety of birdlife is found along the lower parts of the tracks – take your time, keep quiet and stop frequently (allow about 3hr for the round-trip).

The **North End** of the island (about a tenth of its total area) is also part of the Kapiti Nature Reserve though it is managed and accessed separately. Here the main attraction is the **Okupe Lagoon** with its colony of royal spoonbills, though there are also plenty of rare forest birds about, and a new walkway. Adjacent to this northern reserve is a small plot of private land at Waiorua Bay where one of the half-dozen houses offers the only accommodation, run by Kapiti Island Alive (see p.59).

Maori Treasures

56–58 Guthrie St, Lower Hutt, around 15km northeast of Wellington. Mon–Sat 10am–4pm ☏04/939 9630, ⓦwww.maoritreasures.com.

This classy Maori art studio, gallery, shop and café tucked out in the commuter belt is well worth an excursion for the insight it gives into **Maori arts**. There's a real passion for the culture out here, expressed in carving in wood, greenstone and bone, plus painting, basketry, fibre arts, clay works and stone sculpture. Minibuses run from **Wellington Visitor Centre** to the complex where you're welcomed into private studios and then given a chance to watch artists at work, learn something of Maori artistic traditions and customs, touch a kiwi-feather cloak and make a flax souvenir.

Mountain biking in the Wellington region

Karapoti is in the Akatarawa forest 10km northwest of Upper Hutt. ⓦwww.karapoti.co.nz. Makara Peak is 8km west of central Wellington.

New Zealand's most well-known mountain bike race is the **Karapoti Classic**, a tough fifty-kilometre mudfest which is being run for the 22nd year in 2007. It was set up by the Kennett brothers, who are legendary in mountain-bike circles for their excellent and long-running *Mountain Bike Rides* book. The race certainly isn't for everyone. Indeed Simon Kennett had his tongue planted firmly in his cheek when stating "Everyone who rides the Karapoti is perfectly sane. We wouldn't let them race otherwise." Elite riders complete the course in under three hours: mere mortals take much longer but the ride is open to all reasonably strong riders.

To test out your skills and fitness before venturing out, head to **Makara Peak Mountain Bike Park**, a compact area singletrack with a wide range of grades.

Trips and tours

Flat Earth Tours ☎ 0800/775 805 & 04/977 5805, ⓦ www.flatearth.co.nz. Upscale and professional Wellington-based tour company running themed guided trips around the region. The best are their full-day Wild Wellington trip ($275), which includes a 4WD trip along the coast to The Red Rocks seal colony, and the full-day The Lord of the Rings tour ($275) calling at several filming locations and places where the stars hung out.

Kapiti Island Alive ☎ 06/364 8818, ⓦ www.kapitiislandalive.co.nz. Nature and heritage tours to Kapiti Island, staying at the northern end at Kapiti Nature Lodge, the only accommodation on the island. Being Maori-run there's a communal feel which runs through to the modest family-style meals which might include recently gathered seafood. A maximum of ten are accommodated in simple bunkrooms, doubles or twins; take a sleeping bag. Rates are $140–200 a head, including breakfast, lunch and dinner.

Walk Wellington ☎ 04/384 9590 ⓔ walkwellington@xtra.co.nz. The best way to discover the heart and soul of Wellington is on foot. Walk Wellington makes this very easy by giving you a personal introduction to the city. There are a range of speciality walks available.

Nelson/
Marlborough

Many people's favourable first impression of the South Island is formed when they travel to its northern end, and is crystallized by the intricacy of the **Marlborough Sounds**, the sweep of the bays from Nelson as they curl towards **Farewell Spit**, the splendour of the national parks, mountain lakes and streams, the delights of the Marlborough wine country and the natural wonders of Kaikoura. In fact, if you had to choose only one area of New Zealand to visit, this would be a strong contender.

Some of the gentlest but most scenic trekking in the land traces the Marlborough Sounds along the **Queen Charlotte Track**, and with bag transport you may want to pick up a bottle or two of wine a few kilometres south in the **Marlborough wine region**. To the west, the great sweep of Golden Bay arcs out to the point of **Farewell Spit**, a slender nature reserve visited on 4WD tours along the beach. It is wild country, completely at odds with the crystalline aquatic world of nearby **Waikoropupu Springs**. The laid-back small city of Nelson is the best base in the area, with easy access to the wacky **World of WearableArt** museum, and bus transport to the relatively little-visited **Nelson Lakes National Park**.

Most people heading south towards Christchurch will go via Kaikoura with its hugely popular whale-watching and dolphin-swimming trips, but the **Molesworth Road** provides a seasonal off-the-beaten-track alternative taking you through New Zealand's largest high-country sheep farm.

Queen Charlotte Track

Marlborough Sounds Ⓦwww.qctrack.co.nz; access by water taxi from Picton with boat transfer and bag-carrying packages from $65; also guided walks (see p.65).

The **Queen Charlotte Track** (71km one way; 3–5 days; open all year) is a tramping track for people who aren't into tramping. It is a spectacularly beautiful walk, partly tracing skyline ridges with wonderful views across dense coastal forest to the waters of Queen Charlotte and Kenepuru sounds on either side. What distinguishes it from all other multi-day tramps in New Zealand is that you can stay in a range of top-notch backpacker hostels and classy lodges, all superbly sited. Water taxis **transport your bags** to your next destination each day, making hiking a thoroughly pleasurable experience.

Queen Charlotte Sound was an important trade route and provided good shelter and bountiful food for **Maori**. **Captain Cook** stopped at Ship Cove, at the north end of the track, on five occasions and made it his New Zealand base, spending over 100 days there between 1770 and 1777. The shelter and fresh water made it an ideal spot, and plentiful supplies of what became known as Cook's scurvy grass were particularly valued for the vitamin C content.

Marlborough wine region

On the plains and slopes around Blenheim.

If you know anything at all about New Zealand wine you'll have heard of Cloudy Bay's Marlborough Sauvignon Blanc, the wine that put Kiwi viticulture on the international map

61

in the late 1980s. It is still Cloudy Bay's flagship wine and it can be tasted along with a range of their other top-notch offerings.

With around forty percent of the national grape crop, the **Marlborough wine region** dominates the industry. The gravel plains that flank the Wairau River are sheltered by the protective hills of the Richmond Range, and bask in around 2400 hours of sunshine a year making it perfect for ripening the grapes for its esteemed Sauvignon Blanc. Chardonnay and Pinot Noir grapes also grow well, almost guaranteeing tasty bubbly. In recent years, the wineries have been going all out to attract visitors using distinctive **architecture**, posh **restaurants**, art and gourmet foodstuffs as lures. The profusion of weekend visitors from Nelson, Wellington and further afield has spawned a number of classy B&Bs throughout the district, all trying to out-luxury one another.

Montana effectively kicked off the wine region in the early 1970s and now operate **Montana Brancott**, the country's largest winery. Their hour-long winery tour ($10) is a great introduction to the area and the place to learn a little wine appreciation. Of course they offer tastings (some wines free, others for a small fee) and there's a good café too.

Kenepuru Sound

Marlborough Sounds. Accessible from Havelock, 35km west of Picton.

The Marlborough Sounds seldom feel busy, but if it's isolation you want, then head for **Kenepuru Sound**, a series of slender drowned valleys with all manner of nooks and crannies that are perfect for exploration by kayak.

If you're looking for excellent bush-walking with few fellow travellers, consider the **Nydia Track** (27km one way; 2 days), best tackled from the small town of Havelock. It follows a series of bridle paths, making its way through pasture, shrubland and virgin forest, with great views from the Kaiuma Saddle (387m) and Nydia Saddle (347m), as well as along the head of Nydia Bay. The first day (5–6hr) is pleasant, but the second (4–5hr) is the real gem. **Mountain biking** is allowed on the track, but it is a fairly tough proposition in the dry, and near impossible when wet.

Farewell Spit

The northern tip of the South Island, 150km north of Nelson. Access by 4WD tour (see p.65).

At the end of Captain Cook's first voyage of discovery in 1770 he bid adieu to New Zealand from **Farewell Spit**, a slender thread of sand that curls 25km out into Golden Bay. Debris sluiced out of flooding West Coast rivers is carried by coastal currents and deposited here to form an uninterrupted desert of sand, whose shores capture much of the windblown sand from the spit's exposed side. The whole vast sand bank is a **nature reserve**, with saltmarshes, open mudflats, freshwater brackish lakes and bare dunes providing habitats for over a hundred bird species: bartailed godwit, wrybill, long-billed curlew etc. Sadly, the unusual shape of the coastline seems to fool whales' navigation systems, and beachings are common.

The first couple of kilometres of the spit are open for hiking, and if you follow one of the tracks around the base of the spit, you might well come across the wasting carcass of a stranded pilot whale – a sobering sight amid such wild beauty.

To protect shipping, the original **Farewell Spit Lighthouse** was erected in 1870, from materials carried along the spit, and trees were transplanted to the area to provide shelter for the keepers' dwellings. Since being rebuilt in steel and automated, the lighthouse is the destination for Spit tours.

World of WearableArt

7km southwest of Nelson ⓦ www.wowcars.co.nz; Nov–Easter daily 10am–6pm; Easter–Oct daily 10am–5pm; $18.

This museum is a tribute to the annual **World of Wear-ableArt** Awards Show which is now held in Wellington in September (see p.96) but for almost twenty years was the highlight of the Nelson festival calendar. It is a fashion show with a difference, the criteria being sculptures or pieces of art that can be worn as clothes – in many cases made from the most unusual materials such as household junk, food, metal, stone, wood and tyres. The event may be gone but many of the best costumes from past years get displayed here in a manner that owes more to glitzy fashion shows and colourful theatre productions than static gallery or museum exhibitions. Footage of past events brings the whole thing to life.

Nelson Lakes National Park

120km southwest of Nelson.

Widely ignored by international visitors, **Nelson Lakes National Park** is pure Kiwi tramping country. The only real settlement is **St Arnaud**, on the shores of **Lake Rotoiti**, where there are some beautiful easy walks through beech forest. One of the best is the **Honeydew Walk** (30–45min loop; flat) which meanders through beech forest alive with the sound of tui, bellbirds and fantails. Visit in the early evening when the birds are particularly noisy and frisky. The walk gets its name from the sweet excretions of the scale insect which burrows into the bark of the beech trees. It is this that the nectar-loving tui and bellbirds come for.

For something more robust, go for the **Angelus Hut Loop** (2–3 days), which takes you up onto the bald tops. It is a fairly tough slog to get up there but you are rewarded with stupendous views over what seems like half the South Island.

Accommodation is the simple Angelus Hut in the beautiful Angelus Basin with its pretty tarn.

Driving the Molesworth Road

Between Blenheim and Hanmer Springs, inland from and parallel to the Kaikoura Coast; for details visit ⓦ www.doc.govt.nz.

For decades, the leaseholders of the 180,000 hectare **Molesworth Station**, New Zealand's largest sheep farm, allowed people to drive through their property for a few weeks each January and February. The farm has now been bought by the government's Department of Conservation and access is improving. From around Dec 28 to the end of March (7am–7pm only) you can drive through this impressive high-country park, passing historic cob houses with towering mountains all around. The drive from Blenheim to Hanmer Springs (190km) takes over five hours, a couple of them on gravel, and since there are no services makes sure your rig is in good nick and the tank topped up. **Camping** is only permitted at Molesworth cob cottage and Acheron Accommodation (both $6).

Trips and tours

Kahurangi Guided Walks ☎ 03/525 7177, ⓦ www.kahurangiwalks.co.nz. Guided walks on two local Great Walks, the Abel Tasman Coastal Track and the Heaphy Track. Options range from half-day walks (from $25) to the full five-day Heaphy experience ($950).

Marlborough Sounds Adventure Company ☎ 0800/283 283 or 03/573 6078, ⓦ www.marlboroughsounds .co.nz. Professional operators running a number of guided and freedom kayak and mountain-bike trips around the Marlborough Sounds. A one-day guided kayak trip in Kenepuru Sound goes for $95.

Original Farewell Spit Safari
℡ 03/524 8257 & 0800/808 257,
Ⓦ www.farewellspit.co.nz. Operating on Farewell Spit since 1946, these guys run the Lighthouse Safari (5hr 30min; $80), which heads out along the sands of the spit to the historic Farewell Spit lighthouse, all with bright commentary, peppered with local lore. During the day, you'll see vast numbers of birds, seals and fossils, and climb a large sand dune. To see the massive gannet colony towards the very end of the spit you'll need to take the more eco-oriented Gannet Colony Eco Tour (6hr 30min; $105) which includes most of the above plus a 20min walk to the gannets. Departure times are tide-dependant: check the website.

Canterbury/ West Coast

CANTERBURY/WEST COAST | Off the beaten track

T he **Canterbury/West Coast** region spans the South Island and encompasses a huge range of scenery and sights. The eastern seaboard is the more populous and more productive part of the region, home to Christchurch, the South Island's largest city. It sprawls over flatlands at the foot of **Banks Peninsula**, which is formed from two ancient volcanoes, the craters now flooded to form the harbours at **Lyttelton** and **Akaroa**. Inland there's **hot springs**, fine examples of **Maori rock art** and the wild **Mackenzie Country** flanking the mountains.

The Southern Alps run down the backbone of the South Island, both defining and isolating the **West Coast**, a narrow, rugged and largely untamed coastal strip of turbulent rivers, lush bushland and crystal lakes. Seldom more than 30km wide, it comes fringed by astonishing surf-pounded beaches backed by the odd tiny shack or, more frequently, nothing at all. West Coasters, many descended from early gold and coal miners, have long been proud of their ability to coexist with the wild primeval landscape – a trait mythologized in their reputation for independent-mindedness and their fondness for beer. The real pleasure of the West Coast lies in small places closely tied to the countryside, where the Coasters' indomitable spirit shines through: places such as **Karamea** from where excellent trips head out into the limestone world of the **Oparara Basin**.

The region's abundant rainfall fuels the wild **West Coast**

rivers, whose headwaters are visited by rafters flown in by helicopter. The rivers calm towards the coast where jetboats give access to the nesting **white herons** at **Whataroa**.

Windswept Okarito gives a taste of a West Coast town long past its bustling hey-day, but all the better for it. There's a similar tenor at the southernmost point of the Coast where **Jackson Bay** just clings to existence.

Banks Peninsula and Akaroa

Immediately southeast of Christchurch.

Flying into Christchurch only the least observant could fail to be struck by the dramatic contrast between the flat plains of Canterbury and the rugged, fissured topography of **Banks Peninsula**, a volcanic thumb sticking out into the Canterbury Bight. When James Cook sailed by in 1769 he erroneously charted it as an island and named it after his botanist Joseph Banks. His error was only one of time, as this basalt lump initially formed as an island, one only joined to the land as silt sluiced down the rivers of the eastern flanks of the Southern Alps, has accumulated to form the plains.

Today, the two massive drowned craters which form Banks Peninsula are key to the commerce of the region. **Lyttelton Harbour** protects and nurtures the port town of Lyttelton, disembarkation point for many of the fledgling provinces' migrants and now the South Island's major port. It is a workaday town, but interesting for its historic timeball station and harbour cruises. There's an altogether more refined and prestigious tone to the town of **Akaroa**; picturesque and French-influenced on account of its first batch of settlers who arrived from France at the same time as northern Maori and the British were signing the Treaty of Waitangi. Elsewhere on the peninsula, a network of narrow, twisting roads – not least the ridge-crest-hugging

Summit Road – wind along the crater rims and dive down to gorgeous, quiet bays once alive with whalers, sealers and shipbuilders, but now seldom visited except during the peak of summer.

Hanmer & Maruia Springs

140km north of Christchurch. Hanmer pools daily 10am–9pm; $10, two entries on same day $13 Ⓦ www.hanmersprings.co.nz. Maruia pools daily 9am–8.30pm, $10 Ⓦ www.maruiasprings.co.nz.

The quaint spa resort of **Hanmer Springs** is pleasantly situated at the edge of a broad, fertile agricultural plain snuggled against the Southern Alps foothills. Only around 700 people call Hanmer home but the place is awash with holiday homes and, to fully get into the resort spirit, a preponderance of minigolf courses.

The main draw is undoubtedly the **Hanmer Springs Thermal Reserve**, an extensive modern pool complex barely hanging onto a little of its original Victorian charm. While searching for stray cattle in 1859, one William Jones stumbled across the springs which are fed by rainwater that seeps down through fractures in the rocks of the Hanmer Mountains, accumulating in an underground reservoir some 2km beneath the Hanmer Plain. After absorbing some minerals and being warmed by the earth's natural heat, the water rises to the surface via fissures in the greywacke rock.

Similar processes are involved at **Maruia Springs**, 70km west, a small resort in the middle of nowhere with a low-key atmosphere and a range of accommodation.

Maori Rock Art

East Coast, 15–25km northwest of Timaru. Timaru i-SITE visitor centre, 2 George St ☎03/688 6163, ⓦwww.southisland.org.nz; Mon–Fri 8.30am–5pm, Sat & Sun 10am–3pm.

Around five hundred years ago, Maori moa hunters visited the South Canterbury and North Otago coastal plain, leaving a record of their sojourn on the walls and ceilings of open-sided limestone rock shelters. There are more than three hundred **rock drawings** around Timaru, Geraldine and Fairlie, the faded charcoal and red ochre pictures depicting a variety of stylized human, bird and mythological figures and patterns. Some of the best of these can be seen in the region's museums (notably the North Otago Museum in Oamaru). Those remaining in situ are often hard to make out (and require your own wheels), but the best examples are at Risk Shelter, Acacia Downs, Blackler's Cave and Hazelburn Shelter, all northwest of Timaru. They are marked on the Pleasant Point Ward Map available from the Timaru visitor centre, which also organizes access across **private land** to the sites.

Mackenzie Country

200km southwest of Christchurch.

The central highlands of inland Canterbury, along the flanks of the Southern Alps, are now known as the **Mackenzie Country**. The name remembers **James McKenzie**, a Gaelic-speaking Scottish immigrant of uncertain background, who was arrested in 1855 for stealing sheep on a grand scale. He had amassed over a thousand head which he grazed in the rich high-country pastureland which now bears his name.

The region is dominated by New Zealand's tallest mountain, the 3754-metre **Mount Cook**, increasingly known by its Maori name, **Aoraki** – meaning "cloud piercer". Equal star billing goes to the glacier-fed **Lake Tekapo** and **Lake Pukaki**, opaque, pale blue sheets backed by the glistening peaks of the Southern Alps.

The main access to the mountainous terrain around Mount Cook is provided by **Aoraki Mount Cook Village**, which grew at the base of the mountain to cater for nineteenth-century tourists brought here by horse-drawn coaches. You can walk from Aoraki Mount Cook Village to the glaciers lurking beneath Mount Cook's flanks, notably the 27km-long **Tasman Glacier**, fed by icefalls tumbling from the surrounding heavily glaciated peaks. Further south, the plains finally peter out around the gliding mecca of **Omarama** (see p.75).

The Oparara Basin

Northern West Coast, 25km northeast of Karamea.

The finest limestone formations in Kahurangi National Park lie in the **Oparara Basin**, a compact area of **karst** topography characterized by numerous sinkholes, underground streams, caves and bridges created over millennia by the action of slightly acidic streams on the heavily jointed rock. This is home to New Zealand's largest native **spider**, the harmless, 15cm-diameter gradungular spider, and to a rare species of ancient and primitive carnivorous **snail** that grows up to 70mm across and dines on earthworms. Tannin-stained rivers course gently over bleached-white boulders and, in faster-flowing sections, the rare **whio** (blue duck) swims for its supper. If your interest in geology is fleeting, the Oparara Basin still makes a superb place for an afternoon **swim** or a **picnic** by one of the rivers.

In the **Honeycomb Caves**, the lime-rich sediment on the cave floor has preserved the ancient skeletons of birds, most of them killed when they fell through holes in the cave roof. Bones of over fifty species have been found here including those of the Haast Eagle, the largest eagle ever known with a wingspan of up to 4m. Visit on the excellent and educational **Honeycomb Hill Cave Tour** (see p.75).

The two most spectacular examples of limestone architecture lie at the end of beautiful, short bushwalks. The largest is the **Oparara Arch** (40min return), a vast two-tiered bridge 43m high, 40m wide and over 219m long, which appears magically out of the bush. The **Moria Gate Arch** (1hr return) is a little more distant, though the untouched, high-canopy native forest and a magnificent cavern make it all worthwhile.

West Coast rivers

The production line rafting trips out of Rotorua and Queenstown are fun and don't cost that much, but some of the most thrilling and scenic whitewater trips in the world are here on New Zealand's **West Coast**. Dramatically steep rivers spill out of the alpine wilderness fed by the prodigious quantity of rain that guarantees solid flows most of the time. The steepness of the terrain means you're in Grade IV–V territory – constantly thrilling if not downright scary. If you've enjoyed rafting and want more, this is the place to come. Look out for names such as the Arahura, the Hokitika, the Whataroa and the Perth.

Few of these rivers had been kayaked or rafted until the 1980s when helicopters were co-opted to reach them. Most rafting trips still require **helicopter access**, so costs are relatively high, and what you pay will often depend on numbers. Getting four to six people together as a ready-to-go group will save you a packet. The main **season** is November to April but trips run relatively infrequently and you should **book** as far in advance as possible. Several companies run trips, one of the best being **Rivers Wild** (see p.75).

The white herons at Whataroa

From mid–October to late February, New Zealand's entire adult population of the graceful white heron (*kotuku* in Maori) arrives to breed at the Waitangiroto Nature Reserve, by the northern end of the Okarito Lagoon. The sanctuary is near **Whataroa**, but access is strictly controlled and the only way to visit is with the **White Heron Sanctuary Tours** (mid–Oct to Feb 3–6 daily; 2.5hr; $95; booking advised ☎0800/523 456, ⊛www.whiteherontours.co.nz), which include a twenty-minute bus journey, a twenty-minute jetboat ride on the narrow Waitangiroto River, and half an hour observing the birds from a well-placed hide. The forty-or-so nesting pairs of kotuku are supported by slightly larger numbers of royal spoonbills.

Outside the heron season, the Rainforest Nature and Jetboating Tours ($95) follow essentially the same route but concentrate more on the flora, though you'll also see tui and bellbirds feeding on flowering kowhai from August to October for example.

Okarito

In 1642, Abel Tasman became the first European to set eyes on Aotearoa at **Okarito**, a hamlet scattered around the southern side of its eponymous lagoon. Two centuries later, the discovery of gold sparked an eighteen-month boom that saw fifty stores and hotels spring up along the lagoon's shores. Timber milling and flax production stood in once the gold had gone but the community foundered, leaving a handful of holiday homes, a few dozen permanent residents, and a lovely beach and lagoon used as a setting for Keri Hulme's Booker Prize-winning novel *The Bone People*.

The best of the **Okarito Lagoon** is hard to fully

appreciate from the shore and is best explored with Okarito Nature Tours (see p.75). Boating aside, Okarito seems to draw people in, mainly just to laze about and take long strolls along deserted beaches, the most popular being the **Okarito Trig Walk** (1hr 30min return; 200m ascent) at the southern end of town, which climbs to a headland with fabulous mountain and coastal views.

Haast and Jackson Bay

West Coast, 140km south of Franz Josef Glacier.

At the tiny township of **Haast** you're still on the West Coast's main highway, but you feel like you're on the edge of the wilderness. The wild water of the Tasman Sea forms the western horizon, and mountains hem you in on all other sides.

Haast makes a good base to explore the dead-end road south to **Jackson Bay**, a former sealing station that was chosen in 1875 as the site for a "Special Settlement" designed to rival Greymouth and Hokitika. Assisted migrants – Scandinavians, Germans, Poles, Italians, English and Irish – were expected to carve a living from tiny land allocations, with limited and irregular supplies. Sodden by rain, crops rotted, and people were soon leaving in droves; a few stalwarts stayed, their descendants providing the core of today's residents, who eke out a meagre living from lobster and tuna fishing. You can sample the sort of stuff they pull out at *The Cray Pot*, a kind of diner on wheels where you can get fantastic fresh-cooked fish and chips and mugs of tea while watching the sea-tossed fishing boats through fake leadlight windows.

To explore deeper into this region, take an excellent jetboat trip with **Waiatoto River Safaris** (see opposite).

Trips and tours

Black Cat ☎ 03/328 9078,
🌐 www.blackcat.co.nz. To fully
appreciate Banks Peninsula you'll
need to get out on the water. Black
Cat operate two-hour cruises on
Lyttelton Harbour ($49) and groups
can organize special cruises to Ripapa
Island Historic Reserve and Quail
Island Recreational Reserve.

Glacier Explorers ☎ 03/435 1077,
🌐 www.glacierexplorers.com. Go
guided heli-hiking ($285) on the
Tasman Glacier, New Zealand's
longest, with view of Aoraki Mount
Cook, or take a boat cruise ($105)
around its terminal lake where
icebergs carve into the milky waters.

Honeycomb Hill Cave Tour ☎ 03/782
6652, 🌐 www.karameainfo.co.nz/
cavetour.html. Excellent two and a half
hour underground tours where the
interpretation really helps bring the
place alive. $70.

Okarito Nature Tours ☎ 03/753
4014, 🌐 www.okarito.co.nz. Excellent-
value guided kayaking trips either
going for a couple of hours ($65;
minimum two), or overnight staying in
an old hut ($250).

Rivers Wild ☎ 0800/469453,
🌐 www.riverswild.co.nz. Very
professional operation with
experienced guides concentrating on
the fabulously scenic and exciting

Whataroa ($375), the continuously
technical Hokitika ($345) and the hair-
raising Perth ($395).

Southern Soaring ☎ 03/438 9600,
🌐 www.soaring.co.nz. Some of the
world's most spectacular gliding takes
place at Omarama, about 80km south
of Aoraki Mount Cook. Records are
regularly broken here. When the winds
and thermals behave (and they often
do) it is quite possible to fly among the
Southern Alps, especially spectacular
when snowcapped in winter and
spring. Twenty-minute flights start at
$235 but to get into the mountains
you're looking at over an hour ($395).
Also learn-to-fly courses.

Star Watching ☎ 03/680 6565,
🌐 www.stargazing.co.nz. On the
shores of Lake Tekapo Cowan's Hill
Observatory is the place to go to really
see the southern night sky. Evening
sessions begin with a naked-eye
exploration of the heavens before
ducking into the observatory to focus
on the finer detail.

Waiatoto River Safaris ☎ 03/750
0780 & 0800/538 723,
🌐 www.riversafaris.co.nz. A lovely
two-hour wilderness ride that takes
you from the coast into the heart of
the mountains, with the emphasis
firmly on appreciation of the area's
history and scenery. Deep within Mt
Aspiring National Park you'll really get
an appreciation of just how remote
this area is. Daily on demand; $125.

Southern Lakes

Wedged between the sodden beech forests of Fiordland, the fertile plains of south Canterbury, the city of Dunedin and the sheep country of Southland lies the district, a region encompassing **Queenstown**, **Wanaka** and the surrounding **gold country**. Rolling, deserted hills to the east give way to the sharper profiles of the mountains around Queenstown and Wanaka, which rub shoulders with the final glaciated flourish of the Southern Alps. Yet further west you're into **Fiordland**, where over a dozen narrow fissures slice their way deep into the mountains.

Queenstown is undoubtedly the region's jewel, New Zealand's self-proclaimed adventure capital. It can take on the atmosphere of a high-priced theme park but, as ever, scratching the surface reveals a much subtler picture. Wanaka, an hour's drive north, is more laid-back and many prefer to base themselves there, still within easy striking distance of myriad sights and activities.

Arriving from the West Coast you'll pass through Makarora where the **Siberia Experience** gives a wonderful introduction to the region. At the opposite end of Lake Wanaka the resort town of Wanaka is a great base for adventure activities, while remaining less frenetic than Queenstown. Perhaps the best bet is to go **canyoning** in the gullies of the Matukituki Valley then reward yourself with a **wine tour** around the world's southernmost wine region.

All roads lead to Queenstown, including one from fabulously scenic **Glenorchy**, where wilderness jetboat trips and great tramping are the main lures. East of Queenstown the Maniototo is an up-and-coming area largely on account of the **Otago Central Rail Trail**, best tackled over two or three days on a bike. Moving into Fiordland, everyone seems set on seeing Milford Sound. If you'd rather avoid the majority of the crowds, opt for **Lake Manapouri and Doubtful Sound**, an equally spectacular region with a far greater feeling of isolation.

Siberia Experience

Makarora, 80km north of Wanaka. Siberia Experience run by Southern Alps Air ☏0800/345 666, ⓦwww.siberiaexperience.co.nz; $235.

The hamlet of **Makarora** lies on the northern fringe of Mount Aspiring National Park, straddling the wet West Coast and the parched brown lands of the Southern Lakes. There's not much to it, but it is used as a base for the Wilkin and Young valley's circuit, a lovely three-day tramp over Gillespie Pass.

Knowing not everyone is up for such exertion, the canny folk in Makarora came up with the excellent **Siberia Experience**, a kind of four-hour sampler of the region. This starts with a short flight through the mountains to the remote Siberia Valley, from where there's three hours of relatively easy tramping (mostly downhill) to the Wilkin River. There you meet a jetboat for one of New Zealand's best backcountry jetboat rides back to Makarora.

There's also the similar and equally spectacular **Jumboland Wilderness Adventure** ($275), involving a helicopter flight into a different valley, four hours of beech-forest walking along the Wilkin River, and the same jetboat trip out.

Wanaka canyoning

Deep Canyon ☏03/443 7922, ⊛www.deepcanyon.co.nz; Nov–March.

Queenstown dominates the attention of adventure seekers in the South Island to the extent that **Wanaka** seems like a poor cousin, though in fact it has a bunch of pretty exciting activities. Foremost is canyoning through **Deep Canyon**. If abseiling down thirty-metre waterfalls and sliding down eighty-degree polished rock chutes into deep green pools appeals, then this should fit the bill. You don't need any special experience, just a sense of adventure and water confidence – once you start into the canyon, there is only one way out. First-timers usually tackle **Emerald Creek** ($195 for a full day), a narrow fissure where fern-draped verdure envelops you, in complete contrast to the parched landscape of the surrounding Matukituki Valley. Half-time tea and biscuits are served mid-canyon, and the day is rounded off with a fine picnic and strong camp-brewed coffee. The main alternative is the **Niger Stream**, which can be used for first-timers ($195), though those after a more full-on experience can opt for the longer and tougher section, **Big Nige** (8hr; $260).

Central Otago wineries

25km east of Queenstown, and around Cromwell, a further 30km east.

Grapes have been grown commercially in the **Central Otago** district for a little over twenty years, but local winemakers have already garnered a shelf-full of awards. Widely billed as "the world's most southerly wine-growing region", the vineyards lie close to the 45th Parallel. Detractors pooh-poohed the area as too cold and generally unsuitable for wine production, despite the fact that France's Rhône Valley lies on a similar latitude. Hot dry summers and long cold winters dictate low yields and high production costs, forcing wineries to go for quality bou-

Cycling around New Zealand

Cycling is an amazing and popular way to get around New Zealand. Surprising really when you consider the unreliable weather, unpredictable wind and the abundance of hills. But there's also light traffic, numerous well-organized camping spots and fabulous scenery, so the pros easily outweigh the cons.

With the 3000-metre peaks of the Southern Alps running down the spine of the South Island you'd imagine it would be the harder of the two main islands to tackle, but a standard loop only crosses the Alps twice and the rest is much easier. Everyone rides the West Coast but after that itineraries are more flexible, perhaps taking in the Catlins Coast in the south and Golden Bay in the north. In the half decade since the Otago Central Rail Trail came into existence it has rapidly established itself as a key link on any South Island circuit, usually approached from Dunedin on the Taieri Gorge Railway (see p.84).

tique wines sold at prices which might seem high ($20–30) until you taste them.

In the early 1980s the Gibbston Valley east of Queenstown was recognized as being ideal for the cultivation of Pinot Gris, Riesling and particularly Pinot Noir grapes. Gibbston Valley continues to develop, but the torch has now passed to sunnier slopes around Cromwell, Bannockburn and Clyde.

Altogether, over twenty wineries are open for tasting, but to fully appreciate the region and the wines you should join a tour such as those run by Appellation Central Wine Tours (see p.81).

Otago Central Rail Trail

100km east of Queenstown Ⓦ www.otagocentralrailtrail.co.nz.

The Southern Lakes region is bounded in the east by the

Maniototo, a generic name for the flat, high country shared by three shallow valleys and the low craggy ranges that separate them. One of the finest ways to explore the Maniototo is on the **Otago Central Rail Trail**, a largely flat 150km route that's open to walkers, cyclists and horse-riders. It follows the trackbed of the former Otago Central Branch railway line and includes modified rail bridges and viaducts (several spanning over 100m), beautiful valleys and long agricultural plains. Opened in February 2000, the trail has since galvanized a dying region and accommodation, pubs and cafés have sprung up to cater to cyclists' needs.

The route is generally hard-packed earth and gravel making it possible to ride most bikes, though fat tyres make for a more comfortable ride. The whole trail takes most people 3–7 days, but if you're just out to pick the choicest bits (or are walking and don't fancy the whole thing) aim for a couple of 10km stretches, both with tunnels, viaducts and interesting rock formations: Lauder–Auripo in the northern section and Daisybank–Hyde in the east. A torch is handy (though not essential) for the tunnels. **Trail Journeys** (see opposite) offer both escorted and non-escorted tours. All equipment (including cycles) can be hired.

Lake Manapouri and Doubtful Sound

180km southwest of Queenstown. Real Journeys ☎03/249 6602 & ☎0800/656 502; 🖅www.realjourneys.co.nz.

The scattered community of **Manapouri** drapes itself prettily around the shores of the lake of the same name, which in the 1960s became a cause célèbre for conservationists: they successfully campaigned against the raising of the lake level as part of the massive West Arm hydroelectric power scheme.

Real Journeys run a cruise across Lake Manapouri followed by a bus trip down a long dark tunnel to the **underground powerhouse**.

Lake Manapouri also provides access to **Doubtful Sound**, a place of glorious isolation and pristine beauty. Wildlife is a major attraction, not least the resident pod of sixty-odd **bottlenose dolphins**, who frequently play around ships' bows and gleefully cavort near kayakers. Fur seals slather the outer islands, Fiordland crested penguins come to breed here in October and November, and the bush, which comes right down to the water's edge, is alive with kaka, kiwi and other rare bird species. Real Journeys run cruises out here, or you might prefer to visit on an overnight kayaking trip with Fiordland Wilderness Experiences (see below).

Trips and tours

Appellation Central Wine Tours
☎ 03/442 0246,
Ⓦ www.appellationcentral.co.nz.
Expert guidance around the Central Otago wineries, concentrating on Bannockburn and Cromwell. Queenstown-based tours take in the afternoon Boutique Wine Tour ($135) which includes lunch at one of the four wineries visited. Enthusiasts will want to go for the full-day Gourmet Wine Tour ($175) with a cheese tasting and visit to the Big Picture, a multimedia wine presentation.

Dart Wilderness Adventures
☎ 03/442 9939,
Ⓦ www.glenorchyinfocentre.co.nz.
Trips for pure jetboating enthusiasts. Three hours' jetboating for $159.

Fiordland Wilderness Experiences
☎ 03/249 7700 & 0800/200 434,
Ⓦ www.fiordlandseakayak.co.nz.
Cruise boats can get you out on the waters of Milford and Doubtful sounds, but they are no match for the intimacy of going by kayak. FWE run 4–5hr trips on Milford Sound and particularly worthwhile overnighters to Doubtful Sound ($300) involving idyllic kayaking on the almost silent waters and camping out on the shore where they have set up comfortable, ecological camping sites. On day two you'll paddle back with a satisfied glow and possibly see dolphins.

Trail Journeys
☎ 03/448 8149,
Ⓦ www.trailjourneys.co.nz. Choose from guided or supported cycling tours, mostly along the Otago Central Rail Trail but also venturing cross country through the Maniototo.

Coastal Otago/ Southland

The southeastern corner of the South Island, the **Coastal Otago/Southland** region, contains some of the least-visited parts of New Zealand. These include the attractive harbourside city of **Dunedin**, once the commercial and cultural centre of the country. It remains a seat of learning and culture, influenced by its university and strong Scottish tradition. From here down to Stewart Island, local accents are marked by a distinctive Scots "burr", the only true regional variation in the country. Within easy reach of the city is the inviting **Otago Peninsula**, an important wildlife haven where you can observe at close range a variety of marine life and sea birds, including penguins and rare albatrosses. The **Taieri Gorge Railway** penetrates the schist terrain inland, while to the north large spherical boulders pepper the beach at **Moeraki**.

South of Dunedin is the wild **Catlins Coast**, a large protected reserve reaching towards New Zealand's southernmost city of Invercargill. This is a magical, virtually forgotten region, home to several rare species and offering dramatically varied scenery, from hills covered with dense native forest to a shoreline vigorously indented with rocky bays, long sweeps of sand and unusual geological formations.

There's a similar feel to New Zealand's third island, **Stewart Island**, with its blanket of virgin rainforest offering a tramper's and birder's paradise. Back on the "mainland" the south coast road turns north again near Tuatapere, the starting point for the excellent **Hump Ridge Track**, which crosses some wonderful old wooden viaducts once used by early loggers.

Moeraki Boulders

40km south of Oamaru. Access is beside a visitor centre (daily 9am–5pm) where there's a $2 honesty box.

Like giant marbles scattered on the beach and partially submerged by the tide, the **Moeraki Boulders** are a curious sight. Grey and almost perfectly spherical, some reach almost 2m in diameter, their smooth skins hiding honeycomb centres which are revealed in some of the broken specimens. Despite appearances, the boulders did not fall from the sky, nor were they washed up by the sea, but rather lay deep in the mudstone cliffs behind the beach. As the sea eroded the cliffs, out fell the smooth boulders, the smaller ones soon being souvenired, leaving only those too heavy to shift.

Maori named the boulders *Te Kaihinaki* (food baskets), believing them to have been washed ashore from the wreck of a canoe whose occupants were seeking *pounamu* (greenstone or jade). A reef nearby was the hull of the canoe, and just beyond it stands a prominent rock, the vessel's petrified navigator. Some of the Moeraki Boulders were *hinaki* (baskets), the more spherical were water-carrying gourds and the irregular-shaped rocks farther down the beach were *kumara* (sweet potato) from the canoe's food store. The survivors among the crew, Nga Tamariki, Puketapu and Pakihiwi Tahi, were transformed at daybreak into hills overlooking the beach.

Taieri Gorge Railway

Daily from Dunedin to Pukerangi ($63 return) and Middlemarch ($71 return) ☎03/477 4449, ⓦwww.taieri.co.nz.

The **Taieri Gorge Railway** runs 77km northwest from Dunedin into the high country of Otago, penetrating rugged mountain scenery that is only accessible by train. Constructed between 1879 and 1921, the line once carried supplies from Dunedin 235km to the old gold town of Cromwell, returning with farm produce, fruit and livestock bound for the port. Commercial traffic stopped in 1990, and the bulk of the route was turned into the Otago Central Rail Trail (see p.79), but the most dramatic section – through the schist strata of the Taieri Gorge – continues, now almost exclusively for tourists. It is mostly run by enthusiasts, so if you ask ahead you might even be able to ride with the driver for a spell.

Most people do a simple there-and-back day-trip, but the railway makes an excellent way to start your journey inland towards Wanaka and Queenstown. A bus service meets the train at Pukerangi or Middlemarch and heads to Queenstown, or you can throw your bike in the train and simply cycle away at the other end.

Otago Peninsula

Immediately east of Dunedin; Larnach Castle open daily 9am–5pm; grounds only $10, grounds & castle $18; ⓦwww.larnachcastle.co.nz.

This crooked, 35km-long **Otago Peninsula** divides Otago Harbour from the Pacific Ocean and offers outstanding marine wildlife viewing. The winding but smooth harbourside Portobello Road makes the peninsula easily accessible and offers excellent views of the harbour and the spread of Dunedin against its dramatic backdrop of hills.

At the peninsula's tip is the small headland of **Taiaroa**

Head, a protected area where several colonies of sea mammals and sea birds congregate. Unique among these is the majestic **royal albatross**, which breeds here in the only mainland colony of albatrosses in the world. Also concentrated on the headland's shores are **penguins** (little blue and the rare yellow-eyed) and **southern fur seals**, while the cliffs are home to other sea birds including three species of **shag**, **muttonbirds** (sooty shearwaters) and various species of gull. The peninsula's other beaches and inlets play host to a great variety of wading and waterfowl and, occasionally, New Zealand **sea lions** – orca and other **whales** can also sometimes be spotted.

Although there's ample opportunity to see much of the wildlife without having to pay for the privilege, it's well worth forking out for one or more of the several official **wildlife tours**. They are informative and take you up close while causing minimal disturbance to the animals. Monarch Wildlife Cruises & Tours, Natures Wonders Naturally, The Penguin Place and Royal Albatross Centre are listed on pp.90–91.

The Otago Peninsula isn't all about wildlife, and you should put an hour aside to explore **Larnach Castle**, a nineteenth-century Gothic Revival pile with commanding views across the harbour to Dunedin. More chateau than castle, it was the sumptuous residence of Australian-born banker and politician William Larnach, who spent a fortune on its construction and decoration. Materials were shipped from all over the world then punted across the harbour and laboriously dragged up the hill by ox-drawn sleds before the very best local and overseas craftsmen pieced together the family home. After years of neglect, the castle has been restored. The effect is engaging: grand in design but never overwhelming with few prohibitive signs, family photos on the sideboards, and no audio tours.

Gore

Central Southland, 170km west of Dunedin. Hokonui Heritage Centre, cnr Norfolk St & Hokonui Drive; Oct–March Mon–Fri 8.30am–5pm, Sat & Sun 10am–4pm; April–Sept Mon–Fri 8.30am–5pm, Sat & Sun 1–4pm; $5. Eastern Southland Art Gallery; Tues–Fri 10am–4.30pm, Sun 1–4pm; free.

Kiwis will probably laugh if you say you're going to **Gore**. It has that kind of reputation. But they don't know what they're missing.

The **Hokonui Heritage Centre** contains the visitor centre, a small local-history museum containing some interesting Maori treasures, and the entertaining **Hokonui Moonshine Museum**. The latter details decades of illicit whisky distillation deep in the local bush-covered hills, which began in 1836 and reached a peak during a regional fifty-year-long local Prohibition from 1903. Among notable distillers were the Scottish McRae family, who settled in this area during the 1870s. Despite the best efforts of police and customs, the only people caught in the act were the Kirk brothers, whose cowshed and stills are on display.

Across the street you'll find the **Eastern Southland Art Gallery** which opened a couple of years back and put Gore on the New Zealand art map. Much of what's on show was bequeathed by expat Kiwi sexologist, Dr John Money, who over half a century amassed a wonderful collection of works including some majestic African carvings, notably Dogon horsemen and a pair of life-size Bambara ancestral figures. Local interest focuses on richly coloured oils by Rita Angus; works by Dutch émigré, Theo Schoon, who incorporated Maori iconography into his painting long before it was fashionable; and career-spanning pieces from the private collection of arguably New Zealand's top living painter, Ralph Hotere.

Native wildlife

When humans first arrived in New Zealand less then a thousand years ago they found a land with no land-based mammals. Roles filled by mammals everywhere else in the world were here mostly filled by **birds** which had adapted to fit niches in the ecosystem. With no mammalian predators, many had lost the ability to fly.

Maori soon dispatched the ostrich-like moa, but many other species survived until Europeans arrived and started trying to turn Aotearoa into an antipodean Britain. Deer, goats, rabbits, stoats, ferrets and Australian possums were all introduced and over the next century devastated the New Zealand bush. Many native species died out while others teeter on the brink of extinction.

Few conservationists have realistic hopes of ridding the land of these pests, but in recent years New Zealand has pioneered attempts to clear pests from offshore islands where the distance from the mainland saves them from re-invasion. Many bird species now only survive on these islands, which they share with New Zealand's prehistoric lizard-like **tuatara** and the **weta**, which looks like an especially creepy grasshopper.

With a limited supply of islands available, the latest trend is creating "mainland islands" either by intensive trapping and poisoning in a naturally well-protected valley, or by ringing a piece of land with a predator-proof fence.

With this level of attention, hopes are high for the species that remain, but some populations are still critically low. The kakapo, the world's largest parrot, is currently represented by just 86 birds.

Catlins Coast

100–150km south of Dunedin.

The best way to enjoy the **Catlins Coast** is to take it slowly, absorbing its unique atmosphere over at least a couple of days. From Nugget Point in South Otago to Waipapa

Point in Southland, the wild scenery stretches unbroken, with dense rainforest succumbing to open scrub as you cut through deep valleys and past rocky bays, inlets and estuaries. The coast is home to penguins (both little blue and yellow-eyed), dolphins, several types of sea bird and, at certain times of year, migrating whales. Elephant seals, fur seals and, increasingly, the rare New Zealand sea lion are found on the sandy beaches and grassy areas, and within the mossy depths of the forest are abundant birds: tui, resonant bellbirds, fantails, grey warblers and colourful tree-top dwellers such as kakariki and mohua.

There are scenic splendour peaks at **Nugget Point**, a rugged, windswept promontory favoured by fur seals and sea lions; **Purakaunui Falls**, among the most photographed in New Zealand; the impressive **Cathedral Caves**, their high "ceilings" and deep chambers carved out of the cliffs by the sheer force of the sea; and **Curio Bay**, where an intriguing forest has been captured in stone.

It is only a year or two since the formerly gravel road through the region finally got a hard surface. This will undoubtedly bring development to the region, but for the moment facilities are fairly limited. That said, you can sleep and eat well for the two or three days you're likely to spend here.

Stewart Island (Rakiura)

40km off the south coast of the South Island.

New Zealand's third main island is the small, rugged triangle of **Stewart Island**, separated from the mainland by Foveaux Strait and until recently largely ignored by tourists. With the creation of **Rakiura National Park** in 2002 a full 85 percent of the island is now protected.

Most of the island is uninhabited and characterized by bush-fringed bays, sandy coves, windswept beaches and a rugged interior of tall rimu forest and granite outcrops. Stewart Island's Maori name is Rakiura ("The Land of Glowing Skies") and the jury is still out on whether this refers to the *aurora australis* (southern lights), occasionally seen at these high latitudes, or the fabulous sunsets. With the arrival of Europeans, felling rimu became the island's economic mainstay, supporting three thousand people in the 1930s. Now almost all Stewart Island's four hundred residents live in the sole town, **Oban**, surviving on **fishing** (crayfish, blue cod and paua), **fish farming** (salmon and mussels) and tourism.

Stewart Island justifies taking a little time over; indeed the slow island ways can quickly get into your blood and you may well want to stay longer than you had planned. Many people come for the three-day **Rakiura Track**, one of New Zealand's designated "Great Walks". Others come for unspoilt nature, perhaps sea-kayaking the vast flooded valley of **Paterson Inlet**, visiting the open, predator-free bird sanctuary of **Ulva Island** just off the shore of Oban, or kiwi-spotting in the wild at **Mason Bay** on Stewart Island's west coast.

Hump Ridge Track

Tuatapere, 80km west of Invercargill ☎03/226 6739 & 0800/486 774, ⓦwww.humpridgetrack.co.nz.

The relatively new three-day **Hump Ridge Track** is gradually capturing the imagination of trampers for its hard-to-beat combination of coastal walking, historic remains, gorgeous sub-alpine country and relatively sophisticated huts. Sections are historically some of the country's most interesting as they follow a portion of the 1896 track cut 100km along the south coast to gold-mining settlements around the southernmost fiord of Preservation Inlet. This paved the way for wood cutters, who arrived en masse in the 1920s. Logs were transported to the mills on tramways, which crossed the burns and gullies on viaducts built of Australian hardwood – four of the finest have been faithfully restored including the 125m **Percy Burn Viaduct** that stands 40m high in the middle and has become a star attraction.

You can walk the track independently, paying $45 for each of the nights you spend in two comfortable and well-equipped huts. You'll still need to bring your own sleeping bag and food, so might appreciate the offer of helicopter **bag transfers** ($45 per day), best on the first day when your pack is heaviest and you have to ascend 900 metres. There's also a Freedom Plus package ($445) which includes one night's backpacker accommodation in Tuatapere, full heli-packing, return transport to the track start, hot showers, a sleeping bag supplied at the huts and a souvenir T-shirt. Guided walks are run by Kiwi Wilderness Walks (see below), and there's also an option of adding in a jetboat trip on the Wairaurahiri River with Hump Ridge Jet (see below).

Trips and tours

Hump Ridge Jet
℡ 03/225 8174 & 0800/270 556, Ⓦ www.humpridgejet.com. Excellent wilderness jetboating trips (full day, $160) along 27km of the Grade III Wairaurahiri River from Lake Hauroko down to the coast. The boating is great, and you'll often get time to relax or hike into the impressive Percy Burn viaduct before jetboating back.

Kiwi Wilderness Walks ℡ 0800/733 5494, Ⓦ www.NZwalk.com. Four-day three-night guided walks on the Hump

Ridge Track ($1195) with everything Freedom Plus provides plus all meals, superior accommodation at the huts, hotel accommodation in Tuatapere and return transport from Te Anau or Invercargill.

Monarch Wildlife Cruises & Tours
Dunedin ℡ 03/477 4276 & 0800/666 272, Ⓦ www.wildlife.co.nz. A comfy converted fishing boat with heated cabin and licensed galley is put to good use, spending much of the day out along the Otago Peninsula. Their Peninsula Cruise (9am & 3.30pm; $75) leaves from the wharf in

Dunedin, cruises around Taiaroa Head then drops you nearby (where you can visit the penguins or albatrosses; $35 extra) and finally returns to Dunedin by bus.

Natures Wonders Naturally Otago Peninsula ☎ 0800/246 446, ⓦ www.natureswondersnaturally.com. Personalized adventure conservation tours which involve a lively ride around the head on specially constructed tracks in modified 8WD amphibious vehicles. The trips (1hr; $40), run with unstinting good humour and exhausting enthusiasm, take in penguin-viewing areas, New Zealand fur seals, sea lions and World War II relics.

The Penguin Place Otago Peninsula ☎ 03/478 0286, ⓦ www.penguin-place.co.nz. Award-winning penguin-conservation project where carefully controlled and informative guided tours (90min; $30; bookings essential) take you to the beachside colony. Well-camouflaged trenches and hides among the dunes allow an extraordinary proximity to yellow-eyed penguins, and excellent photographic opportunities. Proceeds from the tours are used to fund the conservation work and a unit that looks after injured penguins.

Royal Albatross Centre Otago Peninsula ☎ 03/478 0499, ⓦ www.albatross.org.nz. From the visitor centre you can join the hour-long Royal Albatross Tour ($28; closed mid-Sept to mid-Nov) which includes an introductory film and plenty of time to view the birds from an enclosed area in the reserve (binoculars provided). The best months for viewing are from April to August, when parent birds leave the nests and return towards the end of the day to feed their chicks.

Ruggedy Range ☎ 03/219 1066, ⓦ www.ruggedyrange.com. A wide range of guided outdoor trips on Ulva and Stewart islands, especially good for organized overnight kiwi-spotting trips to Mason Bay (from $385).

Ulva's Guided Walks ☎ 03/219 1216, ⓦ www.ulva.co.nz. Ulva Goodwillie leads excellent small-group nature walking tours of Ulva Island, after which she was named. Three hours for $85.

Festivals and events

B elow we've picked out the best of the annual **festivals and events** throughout New Zealand. Local visitor centres can tell you more about these, and about the many other events celebrated around the country throughout the year.

January

1st	**Whaleboat Racing Regatta**, Kawhia.
	Highland Games, Waipu (ⓦ www.highlandgames.co.nz). Celebrates the town's Scottish heritage with caber tossing, Scottish country dancing and general carousing.
First Saturday	**Glenorchy Races** (ⓦ www.glenorchy.com). Classic country horse-race meeting in a mountain setting.
Mid-Jan	**Roots (reggae) Festival**, Kaikoura (ⓦ www.kaikourarootsfest.co.nz). Regularly draws New Zealand's top roots and dub bands and occasional overseas acts.
Last Monday	**Citizen Watches Anniversary Day Harbour Blast** – massive sailing regatta on Auckland's Waitemata Harbour.

February

6th

Waitangi Day, formal events commemorating the signing of The Treaty at Waitangi. (National holiday)

Waitangi weekend

Harvest Hawke's Bay
(® www.harvesthawkesbay.co.nz). Vibrant three-day celebration of the region's wonderful wine and produce. Shuttle buses visit most of the major wineries.

First Saturday

Mission Bay Jazz and Blues Streetfest, Mission Bay, Auckland (® www.jazzandbluesstreetfest).

Rippon Music Festival, Wanaka
(® www.ripponfestival.co.nz).

Central Otago Wine and Food Festival, Queenstown Gardens, Queenstown.

First Martinborough Fair
(® www.martinboroughfair.org.nz). A huge country fête: the streets radiating from the central square are lined with stalls selling all manner of arts and crafts. Repeated the first Saturday of March.

Second weekend

Waiheke Island Wine Festival
(® www.waihekewinefestival.co.nz).

Wine Marlborough Festival, Blenheim
(® www.wine-marlborough-festival.co.nz). New Zealand's most highly regarded wine and food festival, with Saturday's events focused on Montana's Brancott Estate. Individual wineries do their thing on Sunday.

Third weekend

Art Deco Weekend, Napier
(® www.artdeconapier.com). Four light-hearted days of merriment extending to guided walks, open-house tours of domestic Art Deco architecture, bicycle tours, 1930s dress picnics, champagne breakfasts, dress balls, silent movies and the like.

Devonport Food & Wine Festival, Auckland
(ⓦ www.devonportwinefestival.co.nz).

Mid-Feb to early March   **Wellington Fringe Festival**
(ⓦ www.fringe.org.nz).

March

Late Feb to late March   **NZ International Arts Festival**, Wellington
(even-numbered years only;
ⓦ www.nzfestival.telecom.co.nz). Class acts from
around the world descend on Wellington for three
weeks of dance, music, theatre and books.

Taranaki Festival of the Arts (odd-numbered
years; ⓦ www.taranakifest.org.nz).

First week   **Golden Shears sheep-shearing competition** in
Masterton (ⓦ www.goldenshears.co.nz).
The Olympiad of all things woolly.

First Saturday   **Second Martinborough Fair**
(see February, previous page).

Mid-March   **WOMAD festival**, New Plymouth (odd-numbered
years; ⓦ www.womad.co.nz).

Pasifika Festival, Auckland
(ⓦ www.aucklandcity.govt.nz/pasifika). Huge Pacific
music, dance, arts and crafts festival which draws
over 200,000 people to Western Springs park.

Second Saturday   **Wildfoods Festival**, Hokitika
(ⓦ www.wildfoods.co.nz). A day of gorging on off
-the-wall delectables – huhu grubs, possum pies,
gorse-flower wine, assorted mammal testicles
– along with more mainstream delicacies, followed
by a lively dance.

Te Houtaewa Challenge, Ahipara
(www.newzealand-marathon.co.nz). Runners try
to emulate the beach-running feats of legendary
Maori runner Te Houtaewa along Ninety Mile Beach.

ck

April

Easter week

Waiheke Island Jazz Festival
(www.waihekejazz.co.nz). Overseas and local
acts, ranging from big bands to boogie, descend on
Matiatia Bay for five days of chilled out jazz.

Royal Easter Show, Auckland
(www.royaleastershow.co.nz).

Warbirds Over Wanaka International Airshow
(even-numbered years; www.warbirdsoverwanaka
.com). All manner of planes of yesteryear perform in
the skies above Wanaka.

Third weekend

Bluff Oyster Festival
(www.bluffoysterfest.co.nz). Gorging on Foveaux
Strait's distinctive delicacy.

Last week

Arrowtown Autumn Festival
(www.arrowtownautumnfestival.org.nz). See
Arrowtown at its golden best with entertainment,
food and wine as distractions.

June

Middle weekend

Fieldays agricultural show, Hamilton
(www.fieldays.co.nz).

Mid- to late

Matariki, Maori New Year festivities
(www.taitokerau.co.nz/matariki.htm).

Late June to early July

Two-week Queenstown Winter Festival
(www.winterfestival.co.nz).

FESTIVALS AND EVENTS | Off the beaten track

July

Mid- to late July

Auckland International Film Festival (Ⓦ www.enzedff.co.nz).

Wellington Film Festival (Ⓦ www.enzedff.co.nz).

September

First full week

Gay Ski Week, Queenstown (Ⓦ www.gayskiweeknz.com).

Second & third weekends

World of WearableArt Awards Show, Wellington (Ⓦ www.worldofwearableart.com). Bizarre costumes in a catwalk setting.

November

5th

Guy Fawkes' Night fireworks

Second week

Canterbury Show week (Ⓦ www.nzcupandshow.co.nz).

Third week

Ellerslie Flower Show (Ⓦ www.ellerslieflowershow.co.nz). New Zealand's top flower and garden show, held over five days at the Auckland Botanic Gardens.

Third Sun

Toast Martinborough Wine, Food & Music Festival (Ⓦ www.toastmartinborough.co.nz). A specifically wine-orientated affair with all the vineyards open, free buses doing the rounds, and top Wellington and local restaurants selling their produce.

December

31st

Rhythm and Vines, New Year's Eve music festival, Gisborne (Ⓦ www.rhythmandvines.co.nz).